THE
STORYTELLING
ENTREPRENEUR

USING STORIES FOR BUSINESS SUCCESS

MELISSA
ADDEY

Contents

Biography

I mainly write historical fiction, and am currently writing two series set in very different eras: China in the 1700s and Morocco/Spain in the 1000s. You can download a novella for free on my website: www.MelissaAddey.com I worked in business for fifteen years before becoming a fulltime writer, during which time I developed new products and packaging for a major supermarket and mentored over 500 entrepreneurs for a government grant-making innovation programme. In 2016 I was made the Leverhulme Trust Writer in Residence at the British Library, which included writing two books, *Merchandise for Authors* and *The Storytelling Entrepreneur.* You can read more about my non-fiction books on my website.

I am currently studying for a PhD in Creative Writing at the University of Surrey.

I love using my writing to interact with people and run regular workshops at the British Library as well as coaching other writers on a one-to-one basis.

I live in London with my husband and two children.

For more information, visit my website
www.melissaaddey.com

Current and forthcoming books include:

Historical Fiction
China
The Consorts
The Fragrant Concubine
The Garden of Perfect Brightness
The Cold Palace

Morocco
The Cup
A String of Silver Beads
None Such as She
Do Not Awaken Love

Picture Books for Children
Kameko and the Monkey-King

Non-Fiction
The Storytelling Entrepreneur
Merchandise for Authors
The Happy Commuter
100 Things to Do while Breastfeeding

For Natasha – both a great storyteller and entrepreneur – with enormous gratitude for making my children happy and my writing possible.

THE BRITISH LIBRARY'S BUSINESS & IP CENTRE

This book has been written in collaboration with the British Library's Business & IP Centre, and was generously funded by the Leverhulme Trust through their Artist in Residence grant scheme, which seeks to foster creative collaboration between artists and host institutions.

The Business & IP Centre at the British Library supports entrepreneurs from all walks of life in starting and growing successful businesses. The Centre provides access to the UK's largest collection of business and intellectual property data, alongside training, expertise and networks, in a trusted and inspiring space, supporting thousands of entrepreneurs and small business owners each year.

The Artist in Residence project has enabled users of the Centre to explore the application of creative writing and narrative techniques as business strategies, actively raising awareness of the fruitful connections among business, creativity and storytelling in both practical and theoretical ways. The residency has also developed connections between the Library's business audiences and other areas of collection specialism, increasing opportunities for interdisciplinary research and encouraging business users to be inspired by the unique items held in the Library's vast collection.

Thanks must go to the Leverhulme Trust for its support of this project, and in addition to the business owners, storytellers and entrepreneurs who engaged with the project by attending workshops and one-to-ones, and generously shared their stories and experiences.

The Leverhulme Trust

Business &
IP Centre
London

BRITISH LIBRARY

Acknowledgements

I would like to say a huge thank you to the Leverhulme Trust for their funding, and the British Library's Business & IP Centre for hosting the position of Writer in Residence. It has been the most extraordinary gift of a year: I have had so much fun, done so many wonderful things and met so many great people through this role. Thank you to Noelle, who built up my relationship with the British Library from the beginning, and a very big thank you to Jess, who said 'yes' and followed the whole thing through. We did it!

Thank you to all the entrepreneurs who allowed me to use them as guinea pigs, especially for creating the process of a Sacred Bundle in workshops and one-to-one sessions: your stories were inspiring and made me both laugh and cry. I appreciate your honesty and the insights you gave me.

Thank you to Andi Cumbo-Floyd and Alison Baverstock, whose different words both arrived just when I needed to hear them.

I am so very grateful to the storytelling experts who gave me their valuable time to chat through ideas, and gave me new thoughts to process. Sue Hollingsworth, Hannah McDowall, Peggy Neuhauser, Maddi Riddell, Paul Wilson, I learnt so much. Thank you. I hope I did your expertise justice. Thank you to Elaine Powell for tips on presentation.

Thank you to Gale at Winskill Editorial for focusing my mind and improving my words, and to the Streetlight Graphics team: you make my writing life so much easier and more enjoyable.

Thank you to Ryan for making all things possible and to Seth and Isabelle for letting Mummy work 'in the library'.

To everyone who said 'wow' when I told them about this residency: you were absolutely right.

Part I The Importance of Storytelling

'Marketing is no longer about the stuff that
you make but about the stories you tell.'
Seth Godin (www.sethgodin.com)

1. Introduction: Why I wrote this book

I'm a writer. I write both historical fiction novels as well as non-fiction books. Before I took up writing full-time, I worked in business for fifteen years, first developing products and packaging at Sainsbury's Head Office and then mentoring entrepreneurs for a Government grant-making programme. I probably met over 500 entrepreneurs in the course of my work. I'd listen to their stories, offer as much useful advice as I could think of to fit their situation and assess them for the grant programme, which mostly meant trying to figure out if I thought they had both staying power and a business idea that would work. I loved the job. I liked hearing people's ideas and founding stories. I liked getting to know the entrepreneurs and understanding what made them tick. I enjoyed trying to find advice for them that I hoped would help them be successful… and I *loved* seeing them do well.

When I switched to writing full-time I became the 2016 Leverhulme Trust Writer in Residence for the British Library's Business & IP Centre. I had spent time there in my former job, running workshops for entrepreneurs and meeting clients, as well as recommending it to the companies I encountered. The residency shaped itself around the idea of storytelling for businesses, which brought together the skills I'd developed up to this point: working with entrepreneurs and storytelling.

I started in the Reading Rooms at the British Library, doing some background research. I must have gone through over seventy books and articles on storytelling in a business context. The thing that quickly became clear to me was that most of the books focused on global corporations and so the advice was not always entirely relevant to smaller companies. Consequently, I decided the book I wanted to write would focus on the needs of entrepreneurs.

I won't even pretend to you that I am an expert in the field of storytelling for business. There are some amazing books on storytelling out there, written by very experienced, wise people and I have listed all the ones I hope will be useful to you in the Resources section so you can follow up on any aspects you find interesting without ploughing through the whole Reading Room to find them! But I do know entrepreneurs from all the years I have worked with them, and I do think they need their own book, written to suit their particular storytelling needs. So here it is.

2. WHY ENTREPRENEURS NEED A STORYTELLING BOOK

Entrepreneurs generally start out as one or two people with an idea. If that idea has legs and the entrepreneur works hard, the business grows slowly and the entrepreneur goes on a journey. It may feel like a *Snakes and Ladders* board at times, but it has certain key stops along the way that most entrepreneurs will recognise:

- pitching their ideas in a business context

- trying to engage with customers

- the great but terrifying moment when they hire their first employee

- the struggle to let go of their 'baby' as it grows and many more.

Storytelling-for-business books often focus on large organisations, using stories, in particular, to facilitate change management and improve leadership. But as an entrepreneur there's not much need for change management in a tiny new business when every day brings a new challenge. And although entrepreneurs do need to learn to be leaders, there's a big difference between leading a vast unseen workforce and leading the two people who sit in your cramped office alongside you, trying to get a fledgling business off the ground.

This book covers some business storytelling basics while staying focused on entrepreneurs whose businesses are still small, and addressing their unique needs. It explains:

- Why storytelling is important
- Where to get your stories from
- How you might use storytelling at each stage of the entrepreneurial journey.

Usefully, we know that people connect better with a person than a business, and so an entrepreneur has a head start, as their business and them as a person are often interwoven in an audience's mind.

There are lots of tip boxes and exercises throughout this book, which offer small ways to help you as you develop your storytelling skills. The book also has some interactive sections, where I suggest you ask yourself questions so that you get the most out of this book. These are based on workshops I ran at the British Library's Business & IP Centre with real-life entrepreneurs, who helped shape this book as it grew. I hope you find them useful.

3. STORIES WORK

If you want comprehensive proof that storytelling works better than a barrage of facts and figures, you can read *Story Proof: The Science behind the Startling Power of Story*, by Kendall Haven (2007). Haven collected and reviewed thousands of pieces of evidence on the power of storytelling and found that every source agreed that stories have a huge power when it comes to teaching and learning. His work shows that using stories has many benefits, including the following four points, which I consider most important to an entrepreneur:

- Stories improve the recollection and comprehension of any information being offered, so that if you are pitching to investors or other key stakeholders they are more likely to remember what you said and understand any information you gave them.

- Stories create involvement and a sense of community: this is crucial when trying to engage your customers and turn them into loyal followers of your brand and products.

- Stories enhance meaning, so that if you are

telling stories to move and inspire people to act they will better grasp the meaning of the story and take from it the important messages you are trying to convey.

- Stories create motivation and enthusiasm for learning: something that can be very positive when passing on the core values of your business to new employees, as well as training existing staff.

When someone gives us numbers and data and swathes of endless information, we can only concentrate for a short period before our minds begin to wander. We struggle to follow what is being said, we may miss something important and then lose the thread altogether. By contrast, we are hard-wired, as humans, to focus better and for longer on a story, even if it is complex. We can follow what is being said more easily, and we remember it for longer. I would bet that you could recount a story from years ago that a person told you, better than you could talk me through a PowerPoint presentation someone made yesterday, even though they no doubt tried their best to fill it with compelling images, numbers, data and other information.

People are entranced when they listen to a story: think of small children listening to fairy tales; people gossiping; viewers gazing at the big screen; listeners glued to radio stories; people watching soap operas (my sister once talked me through more than *ten years* of a character's life on her favourite soap opera to explain why he was behaving the way he was right now in a particular episode).

I used to meet entrepreneurs and listen to their founding stories for a living. I wanted to yawn when they told me they made vegan cupcakes that they thought were better than everyone else's, since people told me this all the time. But I would wake up again when I heard that they had made a deal to cook the cupcakes in a pub kitchen when the pub was closed to save money because they were just starting out. It was something different and special and interesting about them... and it told me a lot about how they were running their business: creative thinking, using their small resources wisely rather than immediately getting their own kitchen when just starting out – an error many would-be entrepreneurs make.

Their stories were what set them apart: I once had six different baking companies on the books and thought they would be similar, but they were *extremely* diverse. Their goals, their foundations, their staff, their *stories* revealed who they really were and how little they resembled one another despite first appearances.

4. What is a story?

You can over-analyse what a story is and end up feeling that what you want to relate might not be right somehow. I've read books that suggest that some stories are not *proper* stories, they are just an anecdote. Or that if you don't use the *right* formula the story won't have any effect on your audience.

This kind of statement can throw anyone into a panic. Are you just telling an anecdote when you thought it was a story? What's the difference? But you are a human being and as such, I think you have an integral grasp of what a story is. You might not be able to explain it very well to me, but you know one when you hear one – and so does everyone else.

I'll illustrate this with my four-year-old son, who asked me to tell him a story. I was somewhat distracted as we were about to cross a road, so I began, 'When I was a little girl, we used to go swimming in the river'. Then I stopped, because my attention was taken up with us crossing the road safely. My little boy tugged at my hand and said. 'That's not a story'. He was right of course. That isn't a story. And you knew that too. It was some information and it might even have been mildly interesting because not everyone has been swimming in a river, but it's not a story. Even a four-year-old knows the difference between information and story. The actual story I went on to tell involved us forgetting the picnic we had made for our day at the river and how good the food tasted when we finally got home and ate it. I thought he would find it funny because children usually find adults making mistakes hilarious.

Having said that, here are a few thoughts on crafting a story:

You need a beginning, a middle and an end. The audience needs enough information at each stage to really grasp the story. If I didn't set the scene at the beginning, you might wonder why we didn't just pop back for the picnic once we realised it was missing. If I tell you we had no car and had walked for over an hour across extremely hilly terrain to get to the river, you can see why no one fancied heading back to get the picnic.

You need to be clear about whether the story you are telling is suitable for your audience and your topic. Your story needs to convey something important to your listeners and you need to know what you want them to think/feel/do as a result. This, for me, is the difference between an anecdote and a story. My river picnic story would be great if talking to a food conference about how much more we value food when we are hungry, and yet how sad it is that many of us never do allow ourselves to be properly hungry before eating and, as a result, often overeat. My message might be: how can we get consumers to really savour food and appreciate it rather than eating without thinking about what's going in their mouths? This would be interesting for the audience and a call to action for them to consider how to achieve this.

The same story would not be suitable for an audience of professional swimmers on the topic of river swimming, because the swimming barely enters into the story at all and there's nothing useful they could take from that story. It might be an amusing anecdote I could tell during the lunch break at the swimming conference, but it would not be a good story for the main session.

So something can be an anecdote in one setting and a relevant story in another. Don't panic. Consider whether the story you want to tell is both relevant to the audience and can communicate what you need it to communicate. **THINK**: will it have the effect you want it to have on the audience? Be clear what you want the audience to do: feel something for your business or products; take action in some way; tell you something, and so on. Will your story do this?

Often people are encouraged to use a 'hero' structure for storytelling, where someone – e.g. the founder of a business – is cast as the hero on a quest, trying to reach their goal. Their ups and downs, highs and lows are listed before they finish on a triumphant or hopeful ending, inviting the listener to get on-board – to invest, buy, follow this hero.

My four-year-old, who often amuses me with his thoughts on stories, pointed out that people are often very sad in a story just before they are happy. And you knew that too, because you've heard or seen even more stories than he has.

If you'd like to see a perfect example of this style of story, take a look at the Glasses Direct website (www. glassesdirect.co.uk/about/jamie-and-kevin). As a student, Jamie Wells needed glasses but was shocked by the £150+ price tag. He spent some time trying to find out the actual cost (retailers were very secretive) and, when he did, realised that he could offer glasses far more cheaply online while still making a profit. Starting from his parents' front room, Glasses Direct is now the largest online retailer of prescription glasses in Europe. I'd really like you to read the story on the link above. The language used in it is perfect for this kind of structure, where the entrepreneur is a sort of knight on a quest, seeking the Holy Grail to share with their customers, and fighting off the baddies as they go along. According to the website text, Jamie even 'fought' off pressure from High Street competitors and early threats of legal action. If you want a model for the entrepreneurial hero story, this is it.

However, I do want to point out that this structure can be a bit overused by entrepreneurs and that Ursula Le Guin, in a wonderful essay entitled *The Carrier Bag Theory of Fiction* (1989) points out that this is a 'hunter' story (a heroic quest) – but that there are also 'gatherer' stories, which are less heroic and more about the everyday; the minutiae of life.

This is actually also of huge interest to audiences today,

who want to know *how* and *why* you do things, not just *what* you do. So, if you are a fashion designer, it might be more interesting to hear about: how you choose fabrics; how you work with clients to create bespoke designs made just for their special occasions; how you have travelled to where the fabrics are made; why it matters to you to have relationships with your suppliers; that you developed an interest in fabrics because of your relationship with an aunt, etc. than how many clothes you've sold and how you are the next biggest thing.

Think about what you are trying to tell the audience and what you would like them to think, feel and do as a result and the right story will shape itself.

Geoff Mead (2014) talks about stories needing:

- all the senses to be engaged
- dialogue
- a beginning, middle and end
- a hero or character to whom the audience can relate and empathise with.

He suggests starting with bare bones – the basic points of the story – and then adding flesh to those bones to create a fully developed story.

It's worth developing a few stories up front that you will no doubt use repeatedly. Here are six good stories to have to hand. Spend some time developing them, practising them and getting some feedback on them.

These will be the ones you come back to time and time again. Part II will help you to find and shape them.

For each one, try to create different versions that take up different amounts of time: 30 seconds; 3 minutes; and perhaps a special 'extended' version that runs to 10 minutes for when your story is the main purpose of the meeting between you and an audience (such as when you are pitching your business).

1. **Your founding story.** This is your past; it's how you came to this moment or how you came to create the business. You can choose where to start and where to end, but generally this story is important because practically everyone you meet will want to hear it. It's worth having a very short, a medium and a long version of this story because that way you can suit it to the audience's attention span.

   As you are the founder of your business (probably) then part of the story is likely to be about you, and this matters too. If you watch programmes such as *Dragons' Den,* where people pitch their business to investors, you'll notice that the investors are often almost more interested in the founder than the business. They know they will have to work with that person. They also know that if the person is a good entrepreneur then it's likely that the business will work – and if it doesn't then the entrepreneur will just come up with another good idea.

The founding story seems to come fairly easily to most entrepreneurs because they've lived it very thoroughly! What you need to do is tell it to a couple of people and ask for feedback. They might tell you there's too much detail in there about unimportant things, or conversely, that you miss out some interesting things they'd like to know more about. Practice with this story to get the timing, detail levels and rhythm right. This story may well be your 'hunter/hero' story.

2. **Your day-to-day (or perhaps weekly) routine.** This is your present. Customers like this story and it tends towards the 'gatherer' structure. They want to know the hows and the whys; the detail that makes your work special. How do you bake the bread? How do you design the furniture? How do you create a new piece of software? What do you feel when you do your work? Do you get lost in doodles of new designs? Do you enjoy the hustle and bustle of the markets at which you trade? Do you love seeing happy customers? What inspires you? Colours? Tastes? Textures? Throwaway comments? Images are good: details of ingredients, materials, suppliers. This is the story they will remember when they are using your product or service.

3. **Your vision for the business.** This is your future. The people who are most interested in this

are likely to be investors or other people that you are seeking to impress. They want great things for you, of course... probably because they are hoping to share in that success. Try to make your vision strong and memorable, but not pie-in-the-sky or full of never-ending grand numbers. There's more about creating a vision in chapter 9, but concentrate on making the vision seem like a real place that you have visited and from where you are reporting back.

Use images or made-up props to bring it to life ('Here's an award we just won for being the best employer of the year!' rather than 'We will be a responsible employer with a track record for inspiring and developing our people').

4. **Your values.** This is likely to be most important for new employees. How can you communicate what you expect from them? It would be better to tell them about the manager who bought her trainee a celebration cake *before* the exam results were announced, thus showing confidence in them (Thank you, Nicki. It meant a lot), rather than say that you expect managers to build up their team members' confidence and belief in themselves.

    Think about the values you need to pass on and how you can show them in story action rather than through words alone. This may also be useful in selling: by sharing your values, you attach those values to your products and people then buy your values rather than just the product.

5. **Your customers' stories.** These show why your business is needed and wanted. They are your proof that what you are doing is worthwhile and is of interest, not only to stakeholders in the business but also to employees – because then they know why they are doing this job – and to other customers that may need convincing. To get these, gather your customer feedback and find ways to pass it on – perhaps through images or words the customers have used directly.

6. **Your team.** This is one for your business as it grows and stops being just about you, the founder. It can either form part of a pitch when impressing people – Between us we have 200 years' experience doing this – or it can be part of your 'gatherer' story, showing who you are as people and why you love this work – In our company that makes musical instruments for kids we all play a musical instrument and on our 'Jam Friday' lunchtimes our office dog howls along.

Top Tip

When you start creating your stories, try the scriptwriter's trick of storyboarding: stick up some post-its or little cards and write the main points or 'scenes' of your story onto each one, using perhaps 6–10 cards. Then consider how you can make each 'scene' stronger and more vibrant for your audience.

If you've got these six stories to hand then you're in a good position and you can add lots more later on. You do need to practise all your stories, of course. You won't be great straight away. Start small and build up. Ask people for feedback and act on it. Be brave enough to give out feedback sheets when you get the chance and ask specifically for feedback on you as a presenter. There are lots of tips throughout this book to help you improve as you go along. Storytellers take a while to learn their core craft… and they keep learning all their lives.

REMEMBER: the goal of a good business story is to make the audience feel something (happiness, desire, anger, need, pain, loyalty) that will trigger the desired reaction in them, so that they take action in a way that benefits your business.

Top Tip

I discussed what happens when you tell another person's story, like your customers' feedback or people whose lives you support through your work, with Hannah McDowall (find her on Twitter:

@storyhannah). She is a professional storyteller who has trained and coached hundreds of social entrepreneurs and charitable organisations to tell stories in pitches and presentations. The stories told are often about the people who benefit from the social enterprise or charity, and you must be very careful not to mis-represent them, their story is theirs and not yours. Much better to tell about how you experienced their story either as they told it to you or as you observed it happening. So the story you tell is your experience of their story: so two stories in one! Another way to ensure you don't take ownership of someone else's story is to invite that person to tell it in their own words, this is very powerful. I used to do this wherever possible for important grant funders when they visited our programme. I would try to get some of the beneficiaries to come in and tell their stories. With food companies, I used to get in some of their products as well, so that the funders could taste their products, because it made the effect of the grants we were providing seem real and tangible.

Other options include:

• Making sure you use their actual words

and phrases (reading out a letter or email; asking the person to write their thoughts so you can use them exactly as they said them).

- Video-ing the person so they can tell their own story.
- Using images of them and their life (where relevant), and so on.

Try not to tell their story as though you own it. Instead, try to make the person come alive in the room, either in reality or virtually. Even hearing their voice say a few words can make them more real to your audience.

PART II WHERE DO YOU GET THE STORIES?

When I was doing research for this book, a key question that emerged for me was: storytelling in a business context sounds great, but where do you get the stories *from* when you are just starting out? Also – importantly – how do you make sure that they are the *right* stories and actually tell you something about the company, share authentic values and engage your customers or stakeholders or employees with the real business, and have not only been chosen because they sound PR-friendly or form an amusing anecdote?

So in this part of the book I'm going to look at three places to get stories from. Each one is useful, but they vary in how personal they are.

5. Stories from outside the business

If you really want to embrace storytelling, then keep a look out for good stories wherever you go. Jot them down in a little book to come back to later, or pop them in a file. Good storytellers always have some stories up their sleeves and also, the more stories you read, the better a storyteller you will become, because you will begin to recognise what makes a good story. You can just jot down the basic points of a story and return to it later to add more detail to it. Here are just a few places where you can find stories:

1. Got kids? Use their fairy tales. Fairy tales have been passed down for thousands of years, so there's something powerful and enduring about them. They are instantly recognisable. They are linked to our childhoods, a time when we were deeply impressionable. You can use elements of them and structure your story around them (perhaps saying that you used to be an ugly duckling and are now a swan… or getting there!). You can use their core structures to build new stories (three attempts

at something before you succeed; being lost in a dark place but having the bravery to befriend strangers who can give you a helping hand), and so on.

2. If faith is relevant to your business then you can use parables or sacred stories if they are right for your audience. Again, this taps into people's beliefs and cultures very deeply, so you might need to think about how and when to use such stories, but they can be very precious when used well.

3. The news can be a good source of stories when you need to be topical in what you are talking about. Big news stories will be known by everyone and can therefore bring a crowd together. Bear in mind that many news stories tend to have a negative slant, however, and that may not be a good thing to align with your business.

4. Celebrities can give you 'shorthand' for what you are trying to say. I used to train food companies about writing the marketing copy on their packaging and when I tried to explain 'tone of voice' I would ask them to imagine Delia Smith and Jamie Oliver's takes on the same recipe instructions. It was a quick and easy way to get them to imagine two very different examples, and to understand what *tone of voice* meant so that they could develop their own.

5. You can use ready-made stories from history books, novels, business books, films, the theatre, music, TV and radio, as well as blogs related to your subject, obituaries and biographies. These can give you the opportunity to introduce a sound or visual clip (be aware that for copyright reasons this might need to be cleared or paid for before you use it), or you could read an excerpt so that your audience can experience the story alongside you if they don't know it already.

   You can use these stories in many ways: to add some humour or drama; to illustrate certain ideas, situations or behaviour; and to set a certain tone or mood. You can even use different adaptations of the same story to show how one story can have many interpretations or ways of presenting a character. The original film of *The Jungle Book* by Disney is quite charming and not very threatening, even when the 'baddie' Shere Khan the tiger attacks Mowgli. The same scene with live-action animals is genuinely frightening.

6. Other businesses can also be a useful source of stories. Their success or failure can be used by you to explain decisions or plans you are making. You can use them for inspiration, or as a cautionary example. There's no need to denigrate them, but you can show how the

choices they made are, or are not, choices that are right for your business.

Top Tip

If you have a tendency to speak very fast – as I do! – then try to slow down sometimes. A group I was working with on this topic identified that many very important people seemed to speak more slowly than average, because they expect people to wait for their words, to not interrupt. It gives them a very strong aura of power and gives their words importance. Pause so that you have time to think and breathe. Slow down your words so that people have a chance to take them in. Be confident that you will not be interrupted. If this worries you, say clearly beforehand that questions can come at the end.

6. Stories from inside the business

Stories from within your own organisation are great because, in collecting them, you have the opportunity to develop a storytelling culture, which means that stories are valued, remembered and shared. It also means that you will be able to generate new stories over time, if you put into place systems for collecting them ongoing. Here are a few examples of ways to create a storytelling culture in your business: you can choose some of these and/or develop ways that work for you.

Individuals and teams

Ask team members to share some of their stories: their childhoods and love stories; their work experiences, both bad and good; their hobbies and how they found them; their values and times when those values have either been trampled on or have shone out. Obviously this goes for you, too!

Perhaps you can have 'storytelling hour' once a week on a given theme with a cup of tea. These small stories may shine a light on team members and enable you to see them better. They may become the inspiration for something new in the business or something you can talk about to your customers: how every member of your team plays a different sport, or loves the same book, and what that says about you as a company. Can you include stories as a regular part of your team meeting agendas?

Pay for staff to receive storytelling training as part of their personal development. This flags up that you value storytelling enough to pay for the skill to be developed. Rather than having the usual '360-degree feedback' when it's time for staff appraisals, you can ask for feedback on each employee, which comes down to two or three stories about them which illustrate some facet of their behaviour or performance. For example, the time they spent all afternoon at the weekend watching the football, while repacking some products into the right coloured boxes because the supplier had made a mistake and there was a trade show on the Monday shows real dedication to the business more easily than saying you think they are 'very loyal to the company and invested in its success' (yawn!).

'What if' stories are ones you'll need to create yourself – or, even better, with your own team). They are your vision for the future, something like Martin Luther King's 'I have a dream' speech, in which he passionately shared his own imagined view of the future when his children would be treated in the same way as white children. When you imagine the business in the future, what do you see/hear/feel? If you're brave, you could have a session with your team to imagine the future of the business, although remember that they may then come up with ideas with which you are uncomfortable! On the plus side, a team that has created its own vision will be much more on-board with making it a reality.

In chapters 7 and 8 you'll read about 'Sacred Bundles'. Perhaps your staff could all create their own Bundles and share some/all of their items with you and the stories behind them. This can give you real insight into your employees and what motivates them, or why they have chosen to work in your business.

Crown a storyteller. Does someone have responsibility for encouraging storytelling? This role could be moved around.

No more PowerPoint slides! Can you include stories in all presentations made, both internally and externally? Be really brave and ban endless PowerPoint slides!

Customers

Southwest Airlines have developed a video storytelling culture, where they regularly post videos showing their customer-service stories: anything from asking singers travelling with them to sing 'Live at 35' (thousand feet) to stories about bridal showers and pizza parties held on-board; looking after travelling pets; and members of the team on their retirement days looking back at their careers (one pilot played the harmonium on his last day while flying the plane!). You can see examples on their YouTube site.

Can you ask your customers for their favourite things

about your business and employees? Is it easy for them to leave feedback? Do you showcase their communications with you, not just in a boring, never-updated 'testimonials' page but as an ongoing venture, in fun and interesting ways?

Ritz-Carlton hotels have a daily fifteen-minute meeting where they simply ask, 'Have you been part of a great customer experience?' thus allowing employees to share positive stories about making their customers happy, with themselves as the hero of the story, boosting their own self-esteem and being praised for their work and attitude.

If you have a chance to meet your customers face to face do you encourage them to communicate with you, perhaps by wearing clothes that prompt conversations (like a t-shirt that says 'ask me where our eggs come from!'), or by asking them questions? You never know when a customer will share a wonderful story with you.

Top Tip

One thing you can do to determine the health of your business as it grows larger is to track the stories that people tell one another about the business and its culture. Are they positive stories, full of humour and inspiration; excited about new products; interested in new people; fond of their customers; and upbeat about their own role in the company (for example, planning to be promoted)? Or are the stories growing negative: disparaging new products and their chances in the market; warning new employees that they don't know what kind of place they've joined; continually moaning about customers and whispering about searching for new jobs? The stories that your employees tell can give you the inside track on your business health.

Ask a new employee to honestly tell you what stories they were told in their first month… you might find out something important about how well your business is doing!

7. CREATING A SACRED BUNDLE

The concept of a 'Sacred Bundle' comes from the First Nations of both North and South America. A tribe would have a bundle made up of items that symbolised their history, values, magical moments, important people and sacred objects. It was treated with great respect and opened with much ceremony, when a person of importance, perhaps a chief or a shaman, would take out items and tell their stories, so that the members of the tribe could relive the history and values of their people. In the West you can see similar ideas in the memory boxes we keep for our children, in scrapbooks and in treasured (but often commercially worthless) possessions handed down from generation to generation.

I first came across the notion in Peggy Neuhauser's book, *Corporate Legends and Lore* (1993), and found both it and Peggy's valuable input via email very interesting. In the USA, a brand-innovation studio called BBMG uses Sacred Bundles with their clients, including Aveda, Sears and Southwest Airlines. Through working with entrepreneurs, I have developed my own process for creating a Bundle.

A Sacred Bundle for a business allows the business to create a collection of items, which together reflect the company's business, its values and vision. This could be a wonderful source of stories for an entrepreneur, because it holds within itself the very heart of the business, and allows you to draw on it for an authentic and powerful way of communicating with others. It can even be used for making business decisions.

I created a set of questions and exercises designed to allow entrepreneurs to create their own Sacred Bundle. It was originally tested on nine entrepreneurs on a one-to-one basis. Each company came in and worked with me individually and we created a list of their Sacred Bundle items. The companies then went away for the summer and created some wonderful real-life Sacred Bundles and these were shown in an exhibition in the British Library's Business & IP Centre.

So that you can get an idea of the kinds of items people chose, I've included all nine case studies as part of this book in the next chapter with a small selection of their items so you can see the variety of choices across different companies. I then went on to run a workshop with a larger group of entrepreneurs to test the ideas further, and see if they could create their Bundles without my direct involvement. It worked really well, so what follows are the steps that you can take to create your own Sacred Bundle. It may sound like an odd idea, but all the entrepreneurs with whom I worked really enjoyed the experience and could see its benefits.

As a result, much of the rest of this book rests on you

having created your own Bundle, because I think it is a very useful tool in creating stories about your business, and dealing with many situations common to many entrepreneurs, so I urge you to try it out.

Top Tip

Making a Bundle can be draining! The Sacred Bundle sessions with entrepreneurs included a lot of laughter and even some tears, as well as the feedback below. Many of the questions can feel personal, because often an entrepreneur and their business are so close they are almost one entity. Thinking about the journey you've taken so far, or the reasons why your business means a lot to you can be very emotional. If you get emotional or very tired, that's a good sign. It means your Bundle is really *sacred* and not just a bunch of random unimportant objects. It can also fire you up, as your core values are touched on and rekindled. All of these reactions are great and a good sign that you are creating something special. Here are some of the comments from the entrepreneurs who had one-to-one sessions:

'I feel dizzy and drained after that.'

'A new way of thinking about and interacting with my business. Genius!'

'Inspiring!'

Figure 7.1: Aztec Goddess Cihuateotl, carrying Sacred Bundles

Step 1: Your founding story

You will need the help of a friend to do this first exercise. If you know another entrepreneur you could do this exercise for each other so that you can both work on your Bundles. Otherwise ask a good friend to sit with you and do this.

1. Tell your founding story. NOT your 'elevator pitch'! Take as long as you need to describe how your business came to be. This will probably take at least ten minutes. Start and

stop wherever you feel is best. Some people start back in their childhoods and end at what happened half an hour ago. Some people start much later in the story and end as soon as they made their first sale. There is no right or wrong. Tell the story the way it works best for you.

2. Your partner should listen very carefully and take as many notes as possible (I don't use shorthand, but I scribble like crazy and try to get it all down when I'm in the listening role). If you are this person, try not to ask too many questions except where you feel something is missing, or you don't understand what has been said.

3. Now the person listening will try to pick out some key items for your Sacred Bundle from what they've heard. It might be moments (you were just eating a yukky ready meal at your desk when you thought *Aha!*); it might be people (your dad and his shed because he made your first prototype or taught you to do something); it might be a feeling or value (the kindness that is important in your shop of clothes for premature babies). It takes practice to hear or spot Bundle items, but even on a first try various things will probably stand out. Things may also NOT be said which your listener can still hear (such as 'family', because a person has spoken a lot about their children, their supportive parents, their idea stemming from

a childhood game and so on). The listener's job is to list all of these things and the person whose Bundle it is should write them down.

4. If it's your founding story, it can seem odd to have someone else pick out items for you, but it is also often insightful. Feel free to add things that somehow didn't come across but are important to you ('Oh, I forgot my aunt who always wore red and I thought she was really stylish!').

5. You now have a list of items which might go into your bundle. If you are working with a business friend you can now swap places and do the same for your friend. If not, you have finished this part. Wonderful! Time for the next exercise, which you can do alone.

Step 2: The many, many questions

This next exercise will take up to half an hour to complete and requires you to answer quite a lot of questions. Try to be very honest with yourself and don't leave out the hard stuff. Answer all the questions. Write quite copious notes, as it makes it easier later. Here are the questions. You may feel that you have already answered some questions because you gave a lot of detail in another question; in that case, refer back to it.

1. Why this business?

2. What is the moment when the business came alive for you?

3. When did you fully commit to it and what prompted that?

4. Is there something/someone that started this in your life?

5. What was your first success?

6. What has been your greatest learning (practical, emotional, business etc.)?

7. What is the thing you enjoy most about running this business?

8. What are your rituals and ceremonies?

9. What do customers mention the most?

10. What people, places, tools, ingredients/materials are involved?

11. What have been the magical moments?

12. Who are the people in your life who have been: your elders/shamans to mentor you; your warriors to fight your corner; your rock/castle to keep you safe; your fools to lighten your spirits; your adversaries against whom you've had to fight or any other important roles?

13. What do you battle against?

14. What is your protection?

15. If your Bundle could only contain (in total) **three** items/events/people/feelings etc. to represent your business, what would they be?

16. What do you want your business to be known for (e.g. values)?

17. What does it mean to you to work in this business?

18. Where is the business going?

19. If you had opened an empty Sacred Bundle on day one of your business and put in just one item, what would it have been? What item would you put in to represent this past year?

20. What are people *actually* buying from you?

Once you have answered all of these, look through your notes. If it helps, use a highlighter pen to highlight items you think belong in the Sacred Bundle. You may notice key people, events, items, ideas, feelings, values and so on. Make a note of them all and add them to the ones you listed in the first exercise.

Step 3: The Grid

I'm including a simple grid you can use. Now your job is to take all the items you've thought of so far and put one in each box. This grid makes me laugh because when people see it they question me very anxiously about it. 'Are there supposed to be sixteen items exactly?' Nope! It's just how I drew it the first time. I even had a weird extra-thick black line along the top, which was cause for even more questions: 'Is the black line where the most important things have to go?' Nope! Just a formatting error!

The grid is just so you can see all your items in one place. You may only have a few items, or you may have more than the grid boxes below, in which case, add your own extra boxes. The number of items is likely to match how long your business has been around. Very new businesses may struggle to have even four or five. A business that's been around for 200+ years will naturally have many more, even if not quite 200! Seeing all your choices together gives you a chance to add, delete, re-name or merge items.

Figure 7.2. Sacred Bundle grid

Top Tip

At this stage, don't worry about *how* to represent the items you're listing for your Sacred Bundle. If you want to put 'optimism' in, or 'wild', then just write that. Later on you can think about ways to represent them in your bundle. Here are some ideas for making the ideas into something tangible:

- A photo of your kids because your product was made for them.

- A scrap of yellow paper because yellow means 'happiness' to you and your business makes you happy.

- A kitchen towel for all the food testing you did in your own kitchen.

- A pebble from the beach where you had your great idea.

- The rival product that drove you crazy – so you invented your own.

- A piece of machinery from the first factory that agreed to make your products.

- The tools that belonged to your grandfather, who started the business.

- Very frequently, founders of a company add themselves to their Bundle, because of course they are key to the business in a way that an employee of a larger organisation is not. You could have some fun with this: customising a doll to look like yourself, or making paper dolls. or even sculpting yourself in Lego or similar.

- Simply writing a word onto a rock, piece of

wood, paper. or even having it embroidered or
otherwise marked out.

Step 4: Reality

Here we go! This is the moment when you can actually
create your Sacred Bundle. There are a few options with
varying degrees of input, depending on the end result
you'd like to have.

- You could just keep your grid as a piece of
  paper with the items listed on it. Maybe you
  can stick it on a wall or have a photo of it on
  your phone for instant reference.

- You can create your Sacred Bundle as a real or
  virtual mood board (Pinterest is wonderful if
  you want a virtual version). Find images that
  represent your items. It might be a heart for
  kindness, a dove for peace or images of your
  family and friends, your desktop and whatever
  else is listed in your grid.

- Or… make the Bundle! Find something to house
  it in (which might be meaningful in itself) and
  put in objects that represent all your items: a
  pebble, seeds, photos, a game board, scraps of
  cloth, a piece of packaging, tools of the trade,
  and more. Once every item is represented, you
  have completed your Bundle.

Find a safe place for it to live. It might be somewhere
very visible in your workspace, it might be somewhere
hidden away. Perhaps it can be entrusted to someone

in the business (the newest person, to then be passed on?), or everyone could take turns with it. You could make it very public (on a wall where all visitors can see it, with a special page dedicated to it on your website), or it could be more private. You could place it in the centre of the table when there are important meetings, as a silent reminder to everyone of the company's values and history. Find something that feels right.

Top Tip

During a Sacred Bundle workshop one woman called me over to her.

'My business started because my husband was unfaithful to me,' she said, 'but I want my Sacred Bundle to be positive. I don't want him in there!'

'I understand that. He'd mess it all up!' I said, and we laughed together before I went on. 'But the Bundle is not a *pretty* thing. It's not an air-brushed version of your business history. It holds the truth. You might not wish to share parts of the Bundle – and you don't have to – but, for example, if your business grows and makes a lot of money and you want to set up a charity to donate some of your profits to, what would be more authentic to your business? To give money to a shelter for kittens because they are cute and PR-friendly, or to a charity that benefits women who have been cheated on and need to find a new path in their lives? The Bundle can help you make choices in your business that truly reflect the history and values of where you have come from and, in doing so, those choices will be stronger and more meaningful.'

When you create your Bundle, don't pretty it up. If there are ugly or hurtful things in it, then they were there, at that time, for a reason. Add them to it. You don't need to use them if you don't want to, but by leaving them out you will have a Bundle that belongs to someone else, not to you and your business.

8. Nine Sacred Bundles: Case studies

What follows are case studies from nine entrepreneurial companies who worked with me on a one-to-one basis to create their own Bundles. I'm very grateful to them for their time and honesty. Their stories were a lot of fun to hear and made the process of the Sacred Bundle come alive for me after a lot of research and planning. I have not included all of their items, just a few from each company so that you can see the sort of items that end up in a Sacred Bundle and the reasons behind their choices.

I hope it will give you some inspiration and insight into the process. These nine companies' Sacred Bundles were created and put on display in the British Library's Business & IP Centre in Autumn 2016. The tip boxes in this section show how creating your Sacred Bundle can often lead on to something else, such as defining your unique selling point (USP), creating new product ideas or even deciding how fast your business should grow.

Exercise

When do you take out the Bundle? Have a little think about when and how it is opened. Is it frequently, at a weekly meeting, to tell one of its stories? This makes it familiar and part of daily life; a chance to memorise all of its contents and to ensure that all the staff can tell the stories as well as you, the founder, can. Or is it very sacred? Does it only come out once a year with much ceremony: telling every story in it, adding something new and toasting it before the Christmas party kicks off? This will make it appear more precious and special, but may also make it irrelevant for day-to-day decisions. You need to find a way that works for you and your business.

1. Desi Doll

Desi Doll is an interactive playmate. Created in both male and female versions, the dolls are designed as educational toys for Muslim children. They recite verses from the Koran in Arabic and then translate them into English, French, Turkish and Malay. The dolls include catchy songs targeted at children between the ages of three and six years, so they can learn basic Islamic teachings. The founder, Farzana, has three children of her own and wanted a fun toy to help her to share her faith with them. Much to my delight, Farzana actually has the original drawing of the doll that she made, before a professional illustrator was brought in.

This item clearly shows the amount of work she'd put into imagining how the doll might work, with buttons on the doll's hands and feet for children to press, bright colours and a friendly face. During our conversation it became clear that family and close friends were key to Farzana's business, and we discussed their representation as perhaps being a large table of food surrounded by a happy family eating together. Not only was the product inspired by her children, but family members and friends had helped her in the early days, such as packing up the dolls into their boxes. But now that the business was growing, Farzana had deliberately not pushed for it to grow too large or too quickly. For her, family and friends came first, and the business needed to come second. By acknowledging this value, we also clarified the role of the business in Farzana's life: it had given her the freedom to spend more time with her family and friends, compared to a previous job she'd held in an investment bank, which left her unable to see her children as much as she wanted to.

www.desidollcompany.com

Exercise

Does your Sacred Bundle contain tips for you as to how your business should grow? Do you really want it to grow very large, very quickly? Or is part of the joy of having your own business that it gives you the freedom to shape your life as you wish, including perhaps growing the business more slowly, or in a new direction? Be open to the story that your Bundle might be able to tell you; the values it might be able to remind you of. It's also an interesting story to tell customers: perhaps you prefer to continue to have face-to-face interaction with your customers, want to stay loyal to providers, or will only allow certain ingredients or materials to be used, and so you deliberately keep your prices high or your delivery times are longer than usual so that you can offer a bespoke product or service. Many people might value this aspect of your business and be willing to pay more or wait longer because they *share* your values.

2. Empatika

Empatika specialises in eco-friendly custom-made fitted furniture. Their founder, Tristan, spent his childhood playing in the woods with his friends and loved making models out of wood. Also as a child, he heard about the Amazon rainforest and the people who lived there, and was distressed at hearing that the rainforest was being systematically destroyed. Today, Empatika not only offers eco-friendly wood and paint options, it also plants a tree for every customer and buys an acre of rainforest for everyone who spends over £5,000 with the company.

When I met Tristan to work on his Sacred Bundle, I noticed halfway through our session that his wristwatch was made of wood; something I had never seen before. Here was a man whose interests and values couldn't help but shine out of every decision he made, even down to his accessories. It was clear to both of us very quickly that wood itself was one of the items in his Bundle. We also ended up identifying kindness as a quality to be included, not only towards the planet, but also in the company's attitude towards customers in trying to understand their needs and satisfying them. I suggested an image of Tristan as a child, to reflect his long-lasting love of nature, while Tristan included one of the rainforest-buying certificates, a cause to which he is committed and which has shaped his business plans to give him a unique selling point.

www.empatika.uk

Exercise

Interestingly, Tristan's love of the Amazon rainforest, which could be dismissed as a personal interest, ended up creating his unique selling point (USP) after having been in business for several years. There are plenty of fitted-furniture companies. What makes Empatika stand out is its commitment to the planet, as well as to the customer. If you feel that your business lacks a strong USP, consider rooting through your Bundle to find what core values it represents, and whether those values might translate into a USP for your business. Sacred Bundles have the power to turn core values into commercial success. Since working on his Bundle Tristan has decided to place even more emphasis on his eco-friendly credentials in the business.

3. Ohyo

Ohyo founder Guy was annoyed at having to buy and then throw away plastic water bottles, not wanting to add to the amount of plastic being consumed and not recycled. However, he didn't want to carry a large water bottle around with him. He found the solution in creating a fold-downable bottle, which decreases in size as you drink the water it contains, thus taking up minimal space in your bag.

Guy's Bundle included the first prototypes of the bottle, which were created with help from his father, who has been a rock to Guy during the development of the business. Families and friends often came up when working on people's Bundles, since few entrepreneurs get going without support from those around them, be that practical, emotional or financial. The element of water itself was discussed, because like Tristan at Empatika, Guy has a natural affinity with his work. He loves to swim in cold water and the first part of his business involved mapping public street-fountains across London. When the time came for Guy to make his Bundle into something tangible, he used a *Snakes and Ladders* board, plotting his entrepreneurial journey across the board from the highs of praise from Prince Charles, who declared the idea 'genius', to the lows of a retailer going into liquidation, leaving him unpaid for thousands of items. The *Snakes and Ladders* board has become part of Guy's pitch to outsiders, showing his journey to date and how the company has done since he set it up.

www.oyho.me

Exercise

Could the shape of your final Bundle actually become a tool you can use when pitching your company? Can you tell your story using the items it contains, or find a way to create the final Bundle so that it becomes a visual prompt? Another attendee at our workshops, who works with fabrics, said she was considering turning her list of items into a wall-hanging that she could show to clients who visited her to have their clothes designed, so that they would understand what drives her and inspires her beautiful clothes.

4. Squid London

Squid London was developed by Emma-Jayne and Viviane, two students at the London College of Fashion. Inspired by Jackson Pollock and by the new fabrics and inks available to them, they created rainwear (such as umbrellas, mackintoshes and rubber boots) in black and white, which changed magically from white to bright colours when they got wet. The range is now available in 25 countries and is particularly popular in shops at prestigious museums of art. A reference to Jackson Pollock was, of course, one of the first items to be put into their Sacred Bundle, and this led nicely onto another moment we discussed – when the two women had rather cheekily claimed to have a meeting with the buyer at Tate Modern. In the ensuing confusion, they did manage to hand over some samples to the buyer, who rang them a week later to say that she loved them and wanted to place an order. Because of their initial Pollock inspiration and their clever targeting of artistically-inclined customers, art museums and galleries are one of their key clients around the world.

Romantically, we could include rain itself in their Bundle, although more prosaically Emma-Jayne mentioned the spray containers they use to test the products when developing them. A bottle of rain water bridged the gap between the two ideas. Remember that it is easy to make your Bundle romantic and PR-friendly but the prosaic reality should also be represented!

www.squidlondon.com

Exercise

Do some of your original inspirations or other items in your Bundle point the way towards ideas for new product development (such as the umbrellas in the Pollock style), or even towards suitable customers (the Tate, MoMA New York, etc.)? Take a look through and consider what new directions or markets your Bundle might be hinting at.

5. Tangle Teezer

Tangle Teezer was the hairbrush inspiration of founder Shaun, a hairdresser with decades of experience behind him, who created a plastic brush which rather than resisting hair, moves with the brushing motion, thus very gently detangling it. The product is now beloved by top models and bloggers worldwide, and is particularly recognisable for the very bright colours in which it is frequently made. The Bundle created for Tangle Teezer included the original black, as well as the bright pink plastic version which were all the factory had available just before a big consumer show that the company was due to attend, before the business had really taken off. Reluctantly, they agreed to have their previously black product made in the bright pink. The product was snatched up by teenage visitors to the show, suddenly creating a bestseller, and proving that even perceived setbacks can lead to something wonderful.

Also into the Bundle went a heavy bronze horse, given to the team by a Chinese contact when the product took off in China, thus representing their global expansion. An unusual but telling idea is the haircut that Shaun still gives every new employee to the business on their first day: a chance to get to know people up close and personal, as well as a return to his core skills which led to the product's first development.

www.tangleteezer.com

Exercise

Is there something in your Bundle that particularly allows you to share core values with new employees? Shaun's haircut for his new team members means that they can experience his skills for themselves, be *literally* remodelled to suit the company and feel personally welcomed by the founder, rather than perhaps seeing him as a distant 'guru'. What one item would you choose from the Bundle to share with your employees?

6. The Hairforce

Head lice can be a nightmare and most lotions and potions no longer work, as the lice have adapted to resist them. Step in The Hairforce, founded by Dee, which offers a detailed de-lousing experience, using both skilled techniques and modern technology over two sessions. Their signature look is one of great glamour, from uniforms modelled on the film *Barbarella* to luxury surroundings in their lounges, all of which were added to the Bundle as we discussed Dee's business.

Dee was one of the entrepreneurs who reacted emotionally when we discussed her business. She said that the relief she saw in some children, who had been miserable because of lice, unable to focus at school or sleep well at night, was truly touching after the process, and made her feel that her service was important. The business works on a franchise model and previous clients had even become Hairforce 'Lice Assassins'. Beloved of celebrities, Dee had piles of both confidentiality agreements she has had to sign, as well as the names of celebrities who love this unique service and are happy to mention having used it, which entered the Bundle via two celebrity books.

www.thehairforce.co.uk

Exercise

Is there a book lurking inside your Bundle? It's one of the questions I ask later on in this book and answer in much greater detail, but in this particular instance Dee would be perfectly placed to write a book along the lines of the classic and beloved series by James Herriot, *All Creatures Great and Small* – except that hers would feature the great and the good and their battles with head lice! Her pile of celebrities in the Bundle would make a gossip columnist salivate.

Is there something in your Bundle that you feel could make a great book? Notice that three out of our nine case studies so far have books of their own: Empatika, Tangle Teezer and Track Surveys; all testimony to how useful a book can be for a business.

7. Track Surveys

Track Surveys was developed by Jo and her co-founder Steve to create software applications to support key talent and HR processes, such as 360-Degree Feedback, performance appraisal, engagement surveys and more. They began as a home-based team of two and some of Jo's initial thoughts around the Bundle were reflective of this, such as presentation folders for an important meeting being chewed by their cat, and a major client calling them while they were on holiday and having to create a presentation they could send to win the bid while abroad.

Fujitsu, one of their first global clients, remained a learning point for them as it represented the steep learning curve they had experienced at the beginning, but also the success they were now enjoying. Jo talked about small-office rituals which might mean little to an outsider, but which amused her and which she felt bound the team together in a shared appreciation for humour and the daily work in which they were engaged: from jokes about it being time for a coffee to unwittingly poetic emails received from customers.

As we talked, Jo mentioned various things that all seemed small, but which actually added up to an overarching feeling of trying to run the business so that they could feel they were part of a 'good world': from paying taxes and mentoring young people to trying to have happy employees. These came together to create a 'feeling part of a good world', which we discussed as part of the Bundle's make-up.

www.tracksurveys.co.uk

Exercise

Do you feel that you are able to express personal and/or business values through your company? If there are values that you hold but are not yet expressed, in what way could you bring them out into the open and make them a part of what your company does? Many large corporations set up or donate to charities, but small companies, as Track Surveys demonstrates, can find ways to live their values through their everyday work. Track Surveys were also one of the case studies that actually involved their whole team in creating their Bundle; an inclusive act which allows employees to feel part of creating the company story.

8. Upcycliste

Upcycliste designer–maker Claire takes chairs and other furniture found on the street, in skips and junkyards and gives them new life, using paints, fabrics and papers. Her work is bespoke, original and very beautiful. Over time she has begun to include more eco-friendly paints and varnishes into her work because that is of importance to her. When we worked through the items entering her

Bundle we found a good luck token of a Cuban banknote from the first café that took on her chairs. A common feature in many Bundles is the 'first-ever customer', whether large or small, who made the founders feel that their business had come alive and that the first customers validated their ideas.

We also discussed the process of 'naming' each piece, which Claire had once enjoyed immensely, as well as delivering the items personally to their new homes, and the care with which people showed her where the item would be located in their house, as though reassuring her that it had found a good new home. Claire had enjoyed these personal connections and wanted them to be part of the Bundle, but had found that, as the business grew, there was perhaps less time for these rituals.

Claire also mentioned a workshop in which she had rented space with 'large red doors' (when developing a Bundle you often hear a phrase being mentioned repeatedly, or are given a striking image which can indicate that this is something of importance to the business), and how she had valued working around other people who shared her interests and values. She had recently set up upcycling workshops where she taught her skills to people wanting to work on their own furniture, and had found a great joy in the feeling of personal connection which came from these, perhaps replacing some of those older rituals as the business grew.

www.upcycliste.com

Exercise

A theme which came up fairly frequently during my work with entrepreneurs on their Bundles was that there had once been elements to the business that they had enjoyed – particularly rituals or personal connections – which had been difficult to maintain over time, owing to scaling up the business, and which they sometimes missed. Ask yourself whether that is true for you and if so, whether you could regain those moments in a different way, perhaps through developing a new element or strand of your business, as Claire did with her workshops for customers wanting to work on their own furniture pieces. Part of the joy of having your own business is to make time for the moments that give you pleasure.

9. Vaughan Memorials

Vaughan Memorials make headstones. Behind them, they have a 200-year-old history, stretching back to when funerals involved horses with black plumes on their heads pulling the coffin. Their current owner Roger can remember being fifteen and woken at night by his father because someone had died and they needed to go and fetch the body. The company prides itself on the care and personal service it offers its clients, with some families using them through the generations.

When I worked with Roger on his Sacred Bundle what emerged very strongly was both the history of his family intertwined with the business, and his sense of service to families. One of Roger's choices was the old stone-carving tools that had belonged to the men who had come before him, and who had told him many stories over the years when he was a boy and young man. These included stories about how, in the past, funeral providers had seen themselves as being part of a group, even if they were rivals in business. If a hearse broke down, Roger told me, a rival would not hesitate to lend his own hearse for the occasion, which showed not only a sense of being part of a brotherhood, but also a respect for grieving families, so that a funeral could proceed without a hitch for the family left behind.

We discussed the possibility of Roger developing a blog to feature these old stories, providing a source of material to engage with customers, while showcasing his own history and sense of pride in caring for families at a difficult time. Roger had in his possession the original bill of sale from when his family had bought the business; a document which mentioned horses and other old-fashioned items of a now-modern business, once again underlining the company's exceptional history as a business.

www.aevaughan.co.uk

Exercise

What is there in your own Bundle that could provide strong material for a blog? Do you have stories stretching back in time, or is your business the sort of work of which people would love a 'behind-the-scenes' glimpse? Could you create a history of your product and the people that shaped it over time – for example, chocolate from the Aztecs to the present day – which would give your customers a sense of the history you belong to? Or can you show a 'day in the life of' from within your business, from tree surgeons to fashion designers? This would let your customers understand what goes on behind your work and help them engage with you as a person. Do you do bespoke designs, which could form a more visual blog and also demonstrate your commitment to making customers happy? Your Bundle can help you to engage better with your customers.

These nine case studies of entrepreneurial businesses show how quite often the contents of a Bundle can be highlighted/employed to find new directions, products, markets and even values, which people have felt unable to express fully. Have a dig around in your own Sacred Bundle and see what you can come up with!

Part III looks at how you can use the stories you have developed from many sources, including your Bundles. Along your entrepreneurial journey, there are many moments when stories can provide the inspiration, confidence or support needed to move forward.

PART III USING STORIES ON YOUR
ENTREPRENEURIAL JOURNEY

How do you know when is the right time to tell a story? You will develop your own intuition for this, of course, but my favourite answer comes from Geoff Mead's book *Telling the Story* (2014), in which he suggests you ask yourself: *Do I need to make this real*? He also lists over twenty situations requiring 'real'. These include, but are not limited to: remembering our roots; encouraging good practice; anticipating change or transition; normalising experience and even, simply, entertaining ourselves and others… one of stories' most important tasks for millennia.

When planning this book, I wrote down some important stages and moments along an entrepreneur's journey and so, in this section, I focus on each of these situations and discuss ways in which storytelling might be helpful in that moment. I also focus on how you might use your Sacred Bundle at those times, to keep your core values showing through in all you do.

Top Tip

How do you begin a story? 'Once upon a time', of course, but this can feel like too much in some settings. However, people go into a different state of being when they hear a story, so you need them to know a story is coming up. You can simply say, 'I have a story', which alerts people to what is about to happen. Try telling a story with and without this introduction and make a note of the audience's reaction. Often, if you announce a story, you can see people relax a little. They change their posture and seem more open. The same will happen once they realise by themselves that you are telling a story, but they will be playing catch-up rather than being ready for the story straightaway. So find the words to announce what is about to happen.

9. Creating a vision

Where are you going with your business? If you don't know, then how will you: a) know when you get there; and b) spot the good opportunities along the way? If you know you'd like to supply a major supermarket with a food product, then you need to know that when a buyer for the food hall of a major department store shows an interest, you should jump at the opportunity. Yes, the volume they want from you is laughable, but the fact is that the buyers from large supermarkets frequently go on 'spying missions' at the food halls to get new ideas, because the food halls are more open to smaller suppliers, and are more likely to have the latest food and drink trends. So you would know that you needed to get into that food hall to impress the supermarket buyer. If you didn't know that was what you wanted, you might decide that the tiny volume was not worth your trouble.

Your vision for the business is a story that you tell. It is your founding story, but with the finale set in the future. It is a bold vision of your success at a certain point in time. You can choose how far to look ahead: at least five years, but possibly ten or more. Here are some questions you can ask yourself to create your future story:

- How does the business look?

- How does the business feel?

- What are you proud of?

- What do your customers love?

- The hard facts (£XX million; XX products; XX countries)

- How big is the company at its ideal size?

- What makes the business special?

- What's the working environment like?

- What is your working day, week, month, year like?

- Does the business match the core values you identified in your Sacred Bundle? These will guide you and may help you to identify your Unique Selling Point (USP).

Remember that like all stories your vision needs detail. Start with the five senses. What does the vision *smell* like (fresh flowers in your office)? What does it *sound* like (laughter of staff on a team outing; busy voices on the phone talking to customers)? What does it *feel* like (smooth oak table in your meeting room), or *taste* like (celebration cake for meeting a huge target)? What does it *look* like (photo with new happy client for your 'wall of fame').

Add characters (your amazing assistant; your wonderful clients; your fantastic loyal team). Allow for some failure (the time the sale fell through but you got a bigger better client), so that you are ready to face the downs, as well as the ups.

You will, of course, have to keep updating this story as time goes by. It is possible that you may have to radically rewrite your story at some point, when something important changes. Perhaps an office will open up in another country. Perhaps you'll have a different product range. Update the story to allow these things to play a part.

Top Tip

Remember that we have five senses and that many people respond better to some than to others. Try to build all the senses into your stories as you develop them, not just one or two. It will make your story really come alive for your audience. Think about taste, touch, smell and visual aspects, as well as auditory elements. Don't shoehorn them where they don't make sense, but try to make room for them all when you can. Ask the audience to imagine certain things (how something might taste), or go one better and pass round things they can touch, smell, taste, listen to or examine close up. I used to talk about how to do taste tests when benchmarking food products, and I used to get the audience to do one there and then with two products I had brought along. It creates a real connection and often sparks comments, questions and feedback you might otherwise have missed out on.

10. Developing a brand or sub-brand

I spoke with Paul Wilson of Make Believe (www. makebelieveuk.com) for this chapter and he talked about brands having once been like a piece of architecture: a planned and created shape, staged and theatrical, and developed entirely by the business. The digital era, he believes, has swept this style of brand away and instead a story is now a better metaphor for a brand. It is dynamic, co-created with the audience, not necessarily logical and can work on many levels. Its 'characters' are also analysed and motivations are important.

You can use story as a strategic thinking tool, visualising what the brand is and where it is going through storytelling. Because of this new collaboration with the audience the story can easily escape: brands can come crashing down because the audience has found a fault in the story; a deceit or a wrong turn; a character action that doesn't make sense. But equally, a story can flourish because of fresh input from loyal customers and their passion for the brand. Paul talked about the importance of every member of a company, from the CEO to the cleaners being able to tell the same story… and yet, how rare that is. Looking back at Track Surveys and how it made a Sacred Bundle as a team, you can see how this would help in creating a story that the whole company knows.

I believe that in creating a brand, you are creating a character in your story. Entrepreneurs may have help with this, in that their company's story is very often their *own* story, and therefore their own character tends to steer the brand. But as a company grows the brand must be able to stand on its own as a character and not rely solely on the founder.

I have frequently had entrepreneurs ask me how to protect their brand and what to do when people try to copy their products. It's true that there are various forms of copyrighting and patenting that you can utilise when trying to protect your brand and products, and they are worth looking into, depending on your industry. However, I was frequently advising food companies, and it is almost impossible to protect recipes in this way. You can keep ingredients a secret, but the truth is that if I bring in a good food developer and a chef, I am likely to crack any recipe in a very short space of time.

In these cases, I made a point of reminding people that having a strong character and voice for their brand can protect them when other wannabees come along. *Your* story is what will stick in people's head and make your product more interesting. *Your* brand is what people will remember and be loyal to, if it is strong enough and stays true to itself. People don't just buy a product; they buy the story that comes with it. And *that* is your brand. In this way, another business will have to not only copy your product but also come up with a better story than yours to convince a customer to switch brands.

A sub-brand, of course, goes through the same process, but also has to belong to the main brand. Think of the main brand as a character and the sub-brands as their children. You should be able to tell that they are related and not spend your time wondering whether they were somehow switched at birth, or are an imposter!

If at some point you change the products or the direction in which you want the company to move, remember that you are going to have to change the story you are telling as well. You can't go from selling cereals to selling cereals *and* shampoo unless you change the story from 'delicious breakfast' to 'feel-good mornings'. And if you do that, you must proceed carefully, as the change in story is a jolt to your consumers. You might be best advised to create a story showing a thought process: 'We didn't just want to make your breakfast great, we wanted to make your whole morning great!'

Exercise

Test out your brand's character. Think up different situations and ask: what would your brand do in that situation? How would it behave, respond, communicate? What would it do that would be different from another brand?

Top Tip

Are you brave enough to risk silence? Sometimes silence is what is needed in telling a story. You can use it to focus people on you at the beginning of your story, to let them reflect at the end and to draw attention to moments of importance in between. It also works very well when an image is being used: rather than babbling over it, let it do the work you chose it for.

11. Developing new products

Because this is an area I used to work in a lot I'm going to look at the basics of new product development (NPD), as well as point out where the storytelling element sits in each stage. When developing new products, there are certain useful stages to work through. Different companies will have their own names or stages, but mostly what they come down to is six stages, as shown in Figure 11.1. Your story is important at every stage.

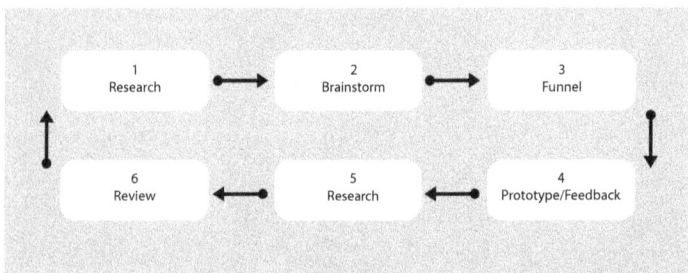

Figure 11.1: NPD Process

Exercise

Does your product have a 'behind-the-scenes' story you can tell people? Many customers really want to know how and why a product was made, especially as it increases in value, or if they perceive that the creation of the product is important to the end result. Kate Newington at Skylark Galleries (www.skylarkgalleries. com), an artists' cooperative in London, told me that when customers come in to look at the paintings on display they always want to know about the inspiration behind each one. The more detailed and complex the story behind the painting, the more likely the customer is to buy it. They not only want to like the image for itself, they want to like the story that comes with it.

Step 1: Research

You need to know your market. This means two things: 1) the people that you think are going to buy these products; and 2) the competition. Who are your customers? What do they want in their lives? What do they enjoy other than your product? What other products do they buy (especially those that they might drop in favour of yours)? The better the research you do, the better you will know your target audience.

I spoke with Maddi Riddell from innovation agency ?What If! that works with its clients to develop new brands, products, services and business models. This stage, researching the market and the customer, is a key part of its work and a process it makes very interesting, through understanding the customer's story. They believe that you need to:

- Know about the customer. Gather data on their life, the 'official' story that people tell you when asked: for example, about their shopping habits – 'Oh, I hardly ever buy snacks for the home'.

- Be with the customer. For example, follow them around a supermarket and note that, in fact, they seem to buy quite a few snacks!

- Be the customer. Actually live an element of their lifestyle to better understand them. While I was at Sainsbury's, one of our teams was working on a gluten-free range, something quite unusual at the time. A member of the team was put on a gluten-free diet despite not having any intolerance to gluten, so that she could see for herself how hard it was to find suitable food. She struggled with breakfast options before arriving one day beaming. 'I've got a great breakfast,' she announced. 'What is it?' I asked. She got out a packet of crisps and an apple, setting off a gale of laughter, but she was truly living the gluten-free customer's story and seeing just how bad their situation could be.

By doing this research, what the agency finds are the human stories going on in everyone's lives, and how products, services or other ideas might fit into those stories. Feelings, locations and experiences all have a role to play in identifying the final story to be told. It is the inconsistencies, the surprises, the laughter and the connections in the mini-stories they find during the research process which, ultimately, lead to innovation:

something which is 'new, true and right for you', as they put it.

?What If! also considers the options for innovation based on three possible levels:

- Now and normal
- Deeper and different
- Weird and wonderful

They use storytelling to share what they have found with their clients, from recreating the bedrooms of three women for the client to understand their cosmetics audience, to keeping a client waiting in their reception until they were enraged… and then explaining that this was the customer's experience of their brand. It's brave to start storytelling when you have an angry client in front of you, but it can also be very powerful!

www.whatifinnovation.com

Top tip

?What If! believes it is crucial to gather the *exact* language and words that its customers use, rather than a vague summary of them. What exact words and phrases and stories have your customers used about your products? What do they tell you about what is important to them about your business?

Step 2: Brainstorm inside and outside the story

It's time to start throwing ideas around. You need a LOT of ideas at this stage, so please don't hold back. Write down every possible idea for a product. It can be ridiculous, it can make you laugh out loud, it can be barely legal (please keep it at least this side of legal!), it can be offensive, it can cost a fortune. It can be barely linked to your current business at all. Just write it all down. Start by yourself, but this could also expand out to a good exercise with your team members. Make sure to write down all the ideas: a big wall of colourful post-its can be fun, or just use a notepad.

Think about your current products and what else you could provide within or outside the story you tell. Obvious links work well, because you can tell the same story. If you do a range of ready-made alcoholic cocktails perhaps you could also sell non-alcoholic versions, or the ingredients for making your own (and the relevant products or services: a cocktail lesson service for hen parties...). Your basic story is, 'We are the cocktail people'. If you change to something wildly different then your story is going to have to change. Why would you suddenly start selling chicken coops? Is it because you're going to become the 'awesome garden' people that make a garden a fun place to be and a real talking point, from colourful cocktails to chicken coops and outdoor sound systems?

Go back a step and take a look at your own and your team's skills and contacts. This is where some of your team storytelling sessions might come into play. Do they have software skills, crafting abilities, musical connections or a qualification in childcare? Can any of these be used for a new range of products?

Also, please do think about products that are not wholly in your control/seem too expensive or difficult to manage. Your task is only to think of ideal products, not the how and where and when. That can come later. I would just warn you about two things: 1) make sure you do your research for your new target audience (especially if it seems to be very different from your current customer); and 2) don't undermine your own brand. If you are known for romantic florals and suddenly create a punk range, you had better be prepared to write a very compelling story to sell your existing customers on the change you've made. Not impossible, but harder work.

Now that you have a tonne of ideas, gather them all up and put them away for at least a week. You can add to them if you suddenly think of something great, but it's important to take a break from this stage so that you come back to them with a fresh pair of eyes.

Top tip

Ask your customers. If they know you for one product and you could offer them another, what would it be? What problems do they have in their lives that they would look to you to fix? It could be interesting to hear stories of problems in their lives and also to note what areas they believe you might be able to help with.

Step 3: Funnel

So, that long list of ideas you made… you can't do all of them. Sorry. It's time to get realistic now and that means you need to throw most of them out. You do this by *funnelling* your ideas. That means a lot of ideas go into the top of the funnel and only a few make it out the other side. Get out the list you made. Take a good look at it and cross out all the ideas you are not really excited about, because if you're not excited about them, I don't see why anyone else should be. Now cross out the ones that really and truly, you're not going to be able to produce right now – because you don't have the skills, connections or cash to make them a reality. For example, a product might be wonderful if made out of delicate china, but rubbish if made in plastic. Don't sell it short because if it's not made properly, your intended customers won't like it either. But don't throw away these ideas. Keep them, because you never know when you might have what it takes to create them. But for now, they will not be included.

Now look at the list you have left. Hopefully it is much shorter. Highlight the ideas you really love and that other people have responded well to. Now think back to that market/customer analysis you did. Do you think your intended customers would like these products? Do they fit the market you've identified? Be a little harsh with yourself and the ideas here. They need to *fit* the market, not be clones. Don't be dull with your products, but don't be so weird that people will just be bemused. By answering these questions you are also shaping the story you are able or willing to tell about your business. Have a last check from this point of view. Are you willing to tell this story? Is it going to need a new story or can your original story accommodate it?

I think you'll now have a very short list. I'm hoping it's less than ten items. I'm impressed with you if it's less than five. Well done! You have some potential new products! Put the list aside for now and sleep on it. Next we'll have a look at what needs to be done to make a real product. Funnelling your ideas is a crucial step towards a great product.

Top tip

Make a few pointers for yourself now about what kinds of story changes are going to be necessary. Will your packaging or tone of voice need to change? Will your social-media message need to change? When you pitch your business, when you present yourself, is there going to be a change because of these new products? In this way, you'll know what else is going to change, along with the launch of your new products. Better to think about it sooner rather than later!

Step 4: Prototype and customer feedback

A prototype sounds kind of flashy, but it doesn't have to be at all. You are simply doing a test-run of the product. This may be getting a t-shirt printed in two colours so you can choose which one looks best before committing to a larger order; or trying the chocolate that will be made into heart-shaped moulds for you. You need to try and see how the real product will look. Sometimes you'll get the exact product, sometimes it's a mock-up. The closer to the final item, the better.

Take a good look at it and ask yourself some questions. Does it look the way you thought? Does it do what it's supposed to do? Does it taste how it was supposed to taste? And so on. If you have doubts about any aspect, then stop the process while you sort it out, otherwise you are just wasting your money. Ask people for feedback and ask them to be as (constructively) critical as possible. Strangers are better than friends for this exercise. If they ask to keep the prototype, you're looking at a promising item! Remember also to look at the packaging the item comes in (does it protect the product and show it off to best advantage?), as well as the ordering process. Is it easy to order? How soon can the customer have it? If you're going to handle the logistics, how storable is the product (does it have a best-before date by which you will need to sell it?), and how much room will it take up. Have you thought about padded envelopes and postage, and how many times a week you'll have to go to the Post Office, or the van you'll need to drive. Or can you get someone to take over the logistics process? These are basic points of new product development but I include them here as a memory jogger.

Now that your new products are getting closer, you can think about including them in your story. Can you start incorporating them now? Can you put out some little hints on your website, your social media, in your presentations about the new direction in which your story is headed or how it is expanding? People like hints about stories that are coming their way; it's why we have trailers at the cinema, and the first chapter of a new book at the end of the one you've just read. It's a little hook to get your customers focused on the next story you're going to tell. I once saw a clever company add a label to their packaging that offered a 'sneak peek' at their new style of packaging that was due out in a month or so. The customers liked being part of the 'club' that got to see the new designs first, *and* they then had no trouble spotting the product on the shelf when its packaging changed.

Top tip

Make sure your product is good quality. A shoddy item will damage your story and anyone who knows about customer service knows that is not good. I once complained about a (newish) oven door having a problem and the customer-service team didn't seem very interested until I said, 'I've been telling all my friends about what a great oven it is and now *this* has happened'. They had an engineer out the next day to fix it for free: they knew that they were about to seriously damage the positive 'story' that I was telling *on their behalf*. By fixing the door, they had the chance to write a happy ending for the story I told in the future: 'There was a minor error but they fixed it right away, and we all lived happily ever after'. Choose good suppliers and check that the product behaves as it should. Be completely happy with it before you press 'go'.

Step 5: Finalise and launch

Make any minor changes needed after having seen your prototype, finalise logistics and marketing materials (if needed). Press 'go'! Once the product is ready, do a couple of test-runs for buying it if the logistics are not in your own hands. If they are, perhaps do a 'soft' launch, where the products are available to a small audience or at a minor event. This is common to make sure everything goes smoothly and iron out any glitches. Once you've got past this phase, consider your products well and truly launched, perhaps at a big event or perhaps with a marketing push via social media. Remember to tell your updated story! This is what makes the difference in your current customers accepting the new products as part of the brand they are loyal to, as much as reaching new customers.

Top tip

If you have a website, use social-media platforms and/or send out regular newsletters or similar to customers, make sure your new products feature on all of those communication outlets and that they are given every chance to develop their own stories. Perhaps have some fun with a new product: use it as a giveaway in a competition; wear it in your profile photo; ask fans to send in pictures of themselves with an item; or even take an item on your travels (a doll/soft toy/sculpture) and photograph it in funny locations. Often later products in a range are not given as many storytelling opportunities as the 'original', so make sure this doesn't happen with yours.

Step 6: Review

Just when you thought it was all over... it very much isn't. From the moment your product becomes a reality, you need to review its performance. Are you happy with how it looks, who makes it and the logistics? What have you learnt that you will apply to the next product? Has the new story given you an idea for another product?

Keep an eye on progress. After a while, does it look dated? Does the product need to be updated? What are your competitors doing? Is it a huge success and should you hurry up and make it in more colours, or provide more options to suit budgets, sizes and individual styles? Is it profitable or are the costs beginning to creep up? Conversely, is there an opportunity to have it made more cheaply while still sticking to your specifications?

When you have a range of products then consider the range as a whole. Is one item more popular than others? Try and work out why and replicate that into the rest of the range, perhaps by tweaking it in some small way. Will the same concept work in a different format (tea towel into coffee cup; notepad into journal)? Is it time to branch out into a similar but different product range?

If you've chosen to create products in collaboration, how is that relationship holding up? Is it time to work with someone else or would you like to develop that relationship further?

How is the story working? Has the consumer taken your original story and applied it happily to the new products? Do they 'get' the connection or are they mystified, in which case the storytelling has gone awry? Does the story need tweaking or making more explicit? Make sure you get customer feedback and, in particular, focus on whether they understand your new products as being part of your overall story.

REMEMBER: when you next get excited about developing an even wider product range, take the time to go back through the six steps of NPD so that you don't miss out on thinking carefully through all the steps necessary to making a successful product… and a successful story.

Top tip

You might like to look at classic out-of-copyright books and illustrations for new product inspiration. The general rule is the author's death date plus seventy years, starting the January after their year of death. So, if they died in August 1950, you wait till seventy years have passed *plus* the next January; ie. January 2021. *Please* check each case separately! The Business & IP Centre can help (www.bl.uk/business-and-ip-centre).

For example, *Alice in Wonderland's* amazing illustrations are now on everything from dresses to teacups, notepads to lampshades. The quotes from the book meanwhile appear everywhere from posters to wall stickers, calendars to business books. In this way you can draw on something well-known and loved to increase your product's desirability. Do stick to out-of-copyright items though, as you can easily end up using material illegally that is not out of copyright.

12. Pitching your business

As part of his job, my husband trains people how to write better business cases; that is, making the case for a business project to be given funding (often many millions). Whereas he does teach them how to value things like time, comfort and happiness with a service, he always emphasises throughout that they *must* tell a story. The person with the power over funding must be taken on a journey, brought into a story that they can believe in, and all the data and numbers in the world will not convince them if the underlying story is lacking. Speaking with Hannah McDowall (Twitter: @storyhannah), who watched many social enterprises bid to be health-care providers, she agreed that even huge health-care commissioners, when faced with a compelling story from a bidder, were far more likely to award business to them than to another provider whose data was good but who seemed unable to turn information on the positive social impact of their work into a human story.

Hannah also pointed out that in business today there is often a trend to tell a story too quickly, to strip it to the bare bones and still call it a 'story'. And yet, as humans, we are able to take in very complex stories and understand them. Complexity is where the details lie and the details are what differentiate your business from another similar business. Allow the specificity of your own voice and story to come through, because your pitch is the moment when the investor or client needs (in a short space of time) to get to know you and assess whether you are someone they want a relationship with: a form of speed dating! So don't rush out a quick overview filled with buzz words that you hope will somehow win over the listener. Instead, focus on revealing who you really are, what your business really stands for.

The reality is that if you reveal the truth and the investor likes it, the relationship will be founded on a strong basis. If you made up a lot of fancy chatter to put a 'face' on who you and the business really are, then even if you win over the audience, they will think you are someone else. It's better to occasionally miss out on a sale or investment than win one that would anyway not have gone well if you were ill-suited. This is like interviews for a job: mostly, if you are turned down, it is because the person interviewing you is aware that you would not fit into or enjoy the company you have applied to.

Remember that I mentioned some key stories you should develop: you will need your founding story for a pitch, as well as your vision, and perhaps add some extra elements; maybe around the experience of your team. Try and make the pitch fun: use props, strong images, perhaps a way of showing your journey visually as Guy at Ohyo does with his *Snakes and Ladders* board.

If you are feeling brave, you can take your Bundle along to a pitch and use it to tell relevant parts of your story. It will allow you to be very honest about who you are, and to showcase your core values and future vision. It will give the audience a clear image of who you are and whether they feel they can trust you, because they will perceive your core values. I was taken aback at how fast I got to know the companies with whom I did a one-to-one Sacred Bundle session. I had spoken to entrepreneurs for years and met over 500 of them and yet I still felt that the Sacred Bundle gave me insights into their business that I would not otherwise have had.

Top Tip

Many people get nervous before they speak, especially if it's an important pitch: their voices go a bit squeaky or croaky. That's great if you do funny voices as part of your story, but not so great for sounding relaxed and confident. Here are three little exercises to help warm you up: go to the bathroom or somewhere else where you can't be seen and try these out.

- Voice: Inhale, then say 'hummmmm-mmm'. Buzz like a bee. Go up and down a bit with your voice, the way you'd imagine an opera singer does their scales (it doesn't matter if you can't sing). Breathe out a few times with a huff; this lets go of a lot of tension. If you can, yell out loud! Open your mouth as wide as it will go. Open your arms really wide and up over your head to stretch your ribs. All of this should loosen up your voice a bit and keep it from getting shaky.

- Body: Bend right over and shake your body about like a loose puppet, as vigorously as you can for at least twenty seconds. Yes, I know your hair and clothes may look messy afterwards. You can fix that. Then roll back up very slowly, setting one vertebra on top of the other till you are standing nice and tall. This exercise shakes out the tension from your body and improves your posture, all in one go.

- Gravity: Finally, put a hand just below your belly button and hold it there for a moment. Focus your energy down to that point; your natural centre of gravity. This stops you getting too 'up' and squeaky with your energy, and instead acts to steady you. Now go tell stories. You'll be great.

Elaine Powell (www.elainepowell.com) specialises in helping people present better and she says that the best thing you can do is to focus on the audience, not on yourself. What do they want? What do they need? How can you give it to them? Focus on their feelings and responses; give them space to respond to your ideas and information. Pause. Pausing allows you to appear in control, poised and confident. Use it to your advantage to take in well needed breath and to swallow if you have a dry mouth. It also allows an audience to digest your content, ask themselves relevant questions, add impact to your content and will give you time to pace your presentation. Make it all about them, not yourself.

13. Making a sale

As an entrepreneur the time will soon arrive when much of your focus needs to be on making sales. Even when you are established you will need to continue working on selling your product. Many of the stories you've already used will help you in this: stories developed around your business and your products are all important, but I just want to add a few examples of how stories can make a difference to your sales.

John Souza, founder of Social Media Magic (www.socialmediamagic.com), quotes marketing expert Seth Godin's advice on sales: 'People do not buy goods and services. They buy relations, stories and magic'. Souza says that he could disagree with this statement only because there are plenty of products that he buys regularly without a relationship, story or magic behind them, but he goes on to say that he would willingly swap any product on that list for a product that *did* have one of those elements behind it, and thus any product he buys which lacks a story is at constant risk of being knocked out of his shopping basket by one that does.

My absolute favourite story about how product + story

= sale comes from the Significant Objects Project (www. significantobjects.com). It was an experiment first run in 2009, in which random second-hand objects were bought at American charity shops. Approximately 100 objects were bought, for a total price of US$128.74. Each item was then assigned to a writer, who wrote a fictional story about the piece (how it was made; how it came into their possession; why it was up for sale etc.). The items were then put up for sale on eBay, alongside their story. The listings made it very clear that the stories were not true. The objects sold the second time for a total of nearly US$3,612.51. The experiment has been repeated various times since then and succeeds in replicating the result every time, lifting the price of an item from an average of US$1–2 up to US$30–40. This is despite the stories linked to the product not even being true. So imagine what your products could do with a good true story attached to them.

Consumers today, especially younger generations – the so-called Millennials and beyond – are becoming more interested in experiences rather than products per se. Witness the recent story about a young couple who spent their wedding funds on a trip round the world rather than a traditional wedding. More and more people want to participate in experiences that they can share with their peers as stories, and so you can see that a product or service that carries a story with it is more likely to be of interest than one without. Make the effort to create stories around your products – the inspiration behind them; how and why they are made; what is special about them; the journey to the customer.

Daniel H. Pink (2014) talks about sales as 'moving

others': in effect, you are persuading people to engage with you: to be moved by your story sufficiently to take action and buy your product. If you want a 'Hollywood' formula for your story pitch you can read Pink's *To Sell is Human,* and use his 'Pixar' pitch, although we've already agreed that there is no need to always use a formula when developing your stories.

So, when trying to sell your products, focus on selling your story. If the customer likes your story, they will like the product and want to have it in their lives.

Top Tip

Take a good look at the products you buy. Why do you buy them? Why not buy another product? Walk round your home and identify at least twenty products, from one-off purchases to things you buy frequently (consumables). Why do you buy each one? Is it something about its story? If you buy many products from one place (your chosen supermarket, for example), why did you choose that supermarket? Do you buy the own-label range or only branded products, or a mix? And again, why is that? What stories do you seem to react best to?

Think about this carefully because you created your product and business, so probably the stories you react well to are stories your audience will enjoy.

14. Communicating on social media

If you want to get serious about your social media then I really recommend a book called *Jab, Jab, Jab, Right Hook* by Gary Vaynerchuk (2013). He talks about using 'native language' on each platform, arguing that just throwing the same information on to every platform, hoping that you're covering all the social-media bases, just doesn't work.

Below are a few hints and tips for each of some major social-media platforms and how you might use your Sacred Bundle to talk the 'native language' for each. A few extra things to bear in mind:

- Always put the name of your company and/or website on to your images so people can find their way back to you, the original storyteller, when they like an image, no matter how far it's been passed on.

- Always make people's life easy when they click your link. If they like the pink sofa with the blue dots and click on the image to buy it, don't lead them to your home page so that they then have to search for the pink sofa again that could be anywhere on your site. Take them to the page where they can click one button to buy the sofa. If someone likes your story, don't start telling it all the way from the beginning again. That gets boring and/or annoying. Make buying from your story *easy*.

- Use images on social media to make your stories stand out. Posts with images are proven to receive a lot more engagement. Use Canva (www.canva.com), a fantastic, easy-to-use, free online design tool.

Jonah Sachs, in his book *Winning the Story Wars* (2012) talks about us being in a 'digitoral era', where digital media means that a new era of oral storytelling has sprung up, where a business can tell its story – but its customers can join in with the storytelling, for good or for bad! So it is important to recognise that in taking to social media, you are joining a group around the campfire and that you must be ready to listen, as well as tell your tales.

Top Tip

A tip for all businesses, but for charitable organisations in particular: say thank you for a sale or donation. It costs you nothing and it makes the customer feel good. I've taken clothes and other items to charity shops and had people barely acknowledge me, which doesn't

> really make me want to donate again.
> Conversely, I donated to Comic Relief on
> their website and the donation triggered
> a brief video of people saying 'thank you'
> from all over the world, from all different
> projects that the charity supports. It was
> actually quite touching and made me
> want to donate more to all the good work
> they were doing.

Some online companies are very smart and while thanking you for the purchase you have just made go on to suggest that you can add to your order in the next half hour for no extra delivery cost. This is an easy way to make people feel that you are grateful for their purchase while not giving you that much more in the way of administration… *and* possibly an extra sale. Consider it the round of applause at the end of an interactive story that has come to a successful conclusion!

Facebook

Big bold images and brief interesting messages with a simple Call to Action.

Facebook, caught up as it mostly is in the minutiae of people's everyday lives – cats; kids off to school; more cats; funny stuff people have seen or heard – is ideal for gathering stories. The minutiae of your business could do well on Facebook if it is presented with strong visual images. 'Choosing new fabrics for the AW collection!' for a clothing company; 'Visit to the people who grow our basil!' for a café; and 'Time to prune fruit trees…' for a tree surgeon's business. Get people caught up in the little soap opera of your business and they will become loyal followers, waiting for another snippet of news from your daily life and happy to communicate with you when you reach out for their input: 'What's your favourite name for the new office dog?'

Twitter

Quick responses, listening, having a strong personal voice for your brand.

On Twitter you can't just tell *your* story; you have to see it as being sat round a campfire where *everyone* can tell their stories. Your job is to listen to the stories and chime in when appropriate. It's a conversation, and a fast-moving one. Ways of joining in include:

- responding fast and 'in character' as your brand when people comment on you or contact you;

- creating polls that people can take part in;

- using trending hashtags such as #FridayFeeling, with something relevant of your own.

Storytelling on Twitter involves being the character (brand) you have chosen to be through and through, and joining in the conversation.

Pinterest

Strong female user-base; boards for planning, dreaming and visualising.

How can your products or services be used in people's lives? Can your bathroom sponges be used in a kids' wet-sponge relay? Take a fun photo and put it on Pinterest, it'll be repinned a lot by people needing ideas for kids parties or summer camps. Are your cakes perfect for weddings? Then create a board around each cake style: romantic; fairy-tale; quirky; goth; modern etc. Brides will get excited by your business if your cake forms the centrepiece of their dream wedding.

Pinterest is about telling stories visually and your products or services will be seized on if they fit into the story someone is telling themselves: their dream body; holiday; car; parenting; old age; clothing; house etc. Your job on Pinterest is to offer your story to help other people tell theirs.

Blogs

Core values expressed meaningfully and engagingly in your own voice.

Not many companies have so many stories that they struggle to tell them all. Many blogs are abandoned after a few enthusiastic months because the business owners run out of good stories because they are knee-deep in the day-to-day work of running a business – and forget that their 'gatherer' stories are interesting. But what if you had 200 years' worth of stories to tell? If you have a business with a meaningful history then your blog could be a wonderful place to share your stories.

Vaughan Memorials have been in the funeral business for 200 years and their blog would be the perfect place for stories showing the shared values and culture of their industry: from craftsmen who worked their whole lives carving tombstones to events such as the annual Undertakers Ball.

If your business is a little more recent, then consider telling the history of your products, ingredients or materials, such as the creation of West African fabrics or the evolution of water bottles from goatskins to plastic throwaways, and beyond, to ecological solutions.

Also, keep your blog honest to who you/your team/ business are; it will be much easier to write if it is. Rude Health, who makes breakfast cereals, calls its blog 'rants' because their founder gets very excited about certain farming and food industry practices and likes to rant! (www.rudehealth.com/rants).

Instagram

Image is everything: be known for something.

What is in your Bundle that could look amazing, that could set you apart from the boring 'look at my product' shots that most businesses upload? Some businesses try to be more creative; for example, by uploading images that they feel express some of their core values –

playfulness, colours etc. But these can vary enormously in subject matter and are not really going to get you known for something unless you are amazingly good at photography. Instead, why not pick something that could engage your customers and focus on it?

Squid London, who make rainwear that changes from black and white to colour in the rain, could, for instance, feature amazing shots of rain, rainbows, thunderstorms, lightning, puddles, raindrops and monsoons. Sure, they could take some themselves – London is never short of a drop or two of rain – but this could also be a good way to engage with customers: asking them to send in their own images of rain. In this way their Instagram feed would become focused around one thing – rain – which is the magical ingredient in their product offer.

Top Tip

Here are just a few small tips for better presentation skills if you're starting out:

- Keep PowerPoint slides simple, with good visuals and not too much text, and if you're really good, drop the slides altogether.

- Props can be fantastic. My sister, who works in academic circles, does presentations where she wears different hats to be the different 'voices' of her research subjects. Her rather sedate audience that isn't used to this style finds it mesmerising.

- Maintain eye contact with your audience.

- Practise in front of someone and get them to tell you if you have any distracting habits (e.g. repeating a particular word or gesture), then work on getting rid of them or toning them down.

- Don't be afraid of using body language; it can be very effective when used properly, if you are acting out a situation.

15. Engaging with your customers

Telling stories should not be a one-way street. A great way to engage with your customers is to ask to hear *their* stories and to showcase them as part of your external communications. Goat's milk company St Helen's (www. sthelensfarm.co.uk) offers dairy products made from goat's milk and on their packs they feature dual stories: their customers' testimonials (with pictures) and the stories of their farmers, including ways to engage with them, such as glamping on their farm. You can imagine that customers would quite like to see themselves – and often their children – on the packs of a product they enjoy and equally, that if you have been to the actual farm where the product is made and had a happy time there that your loyalty to that brand will be increased a hundredfold. Offer a space for your customer's stories: on your packaging, your website, your blog, your Twitter feed.

Firefly Tonics (www.fireflydrinks.com), who make drinks that aim to put a spring in your step, regularly change the images on their labels, running competitions to get new pictures from their customers: people turning cartwheels on the beach or skipping along a wall, showing how the customers are *living* the story the company is *telling*. The same goes for the running experiences that Nike organises, where runners – their customers – meet to run together.

Set up competitions for stories and photos involving your product/service and the customers' experience of it. Can your customers meet you and deepen the story they are hearing about? I know food and drink companies that started on market stalls and that, despite having grown well beyond needing to sell at markets, still attend one or two just to engage with customers so that they can hear their stories and feedback, and tell their own stories directly rather than just through social media. Smoothie drinks-maker Innocent used to mention the Banana Phone on their packaging, which apparently you could ring any time you liked, just for a chat. Could you do something similar? If you can find a way for customers to meet with you face to face so that you can share your stories together I think you will find that those stories will become more meaningful to you both.

Exercise

Quite often business ideas come about because people are struggling with something and then create a solution for it. So don't forget to tell your own story. What made you want to create this product or service? What was going on in your own life? This will often be reflected in your customers' lives and can give you valuable insights. By telling your story, you can encourage your customers to respond with their own stories because they recognise themselves in you.

Top Tip

Getting the audience to step into the story and 'be' one of the characters is a powerful way to make them connect with what you are saying. I used to run a workshop for food companies that wanted to get into the major supermarkets. I knew full well that the audience mostly hated the supermarket buyers, who never returned their calls when they wanted to try and pitch their products. So I always began my workshop by saying that it was a hard life being a buyer, which got a lot of eye-rolling as a response. But I then took them through what life as a buyer was like: often young and without a lot of experience; moving department frequently just as they were learning something; a pizza factory burning to the ground just as pizza was due to feature in a major press campaign; weekly sales meetings in which they were told off if they failed to meet tough targets; as well as receiving (and having to reply to) letters such as 'I make the best Christmas cake in the world but I will *never* reveal the recipe to you as you will only steal it!' from ninety-year-old grandmothers. By the end of this first session the audience was beginning to feel a little sorry for the buyers and, more importantly, starting to understand how better to approach them – e.g. focusing the pitch on their products hitting sales targets and getting a lot of good press and consumer interest. Try turning your audience into the protagonist of a story.

16. Leadership

Denning (2011) says that using good stories as a leader can:

- Motivate others to action by setting an inspiring vision to follow

- Build trust by showing who you are and what values you hold

- Share company values with new staff

- Get people to work together by sharing stories and a common vision

- Share knowledge (and keep it in the business when people leave)

- Tame the grapevine of rumours, scaremongering and other negative stories

- Encourage innovation. Tom Goodwin of Havas Media pointed out in 2015 on Tech Crunch (www.techcrunch.com) that: 'Uber, the world's largest taxi company, owns no vehicles. Facebook, the world's most popular media owner, creates no content. Alibaba, the most valuable retailer, has no inventory. And Airbnb, the world's largest accommodation provider, owns no real estate. Something interesting is happening'. This stacked 'mini story' creates a new narrative which encourages people to look for business ideas in a new way.

I've chosen to pick out two important leader's duties: sharing your values and training new staff. Below are thoughts on both of these tasks.

Sharing your values

When new people come into your business, you need to find a way to share your values with them. You can go through as much historical information of how the business has grown, and wade through current HR policies, but the reality is that none of that helps to share your core values. Two of my favourite stories that I've heard so far about sharing values come from two of the companies I spoke to during the writing of this book.

I gathered some great tips for the Developing New Products (chapter 11) part of this section of the book from Maddi Riddell at ?What If!, an innovation agency (www.whatifinnovation.com). Businesses all over the world come to them to develop new visions, brands, products and business ideas. I had the chance to spend some time with them when I worked at Sainsbury's Head Office and it was a lot of fun. They have very creative ways of working and the ideas they come up were great. The company started out as just two founders in a grotty basement in a disreputable part of town, but now has over 300 employees, housed in offices worldwide. Their

London offices are chic and full of creative touches. How can the founders possibly express to a new employee where they've come from? Simple. They hire a minibus.

When new employees join the agency Matt and Dave, the founders, hire a minibus and take the new recruits on a whistle-stop tour of London. Starting at the horrible old basement and telling the story of their first computers all being repeatedly stolen, they move around the city, showing the sites of all their subsequent offices and storytelling the highs and lows of the early years. By the time the minibus pulls up outside their current offices, the new employees have had a taste of the *real* history of the company, travelling back in time, with the founders as their guides.

Tangle Teezer (www.tangleteezer.com) make a now globally recognisable hairbrush, which brushes without pulling at hair, hence dealing with tangles better. Its founder Shaun is a hairdresser with decades of experience and when a new employee arrives at Tangle Teezer Shaun's first step is to cut their hair. It's a very intimate way to get to know your new boss of course, but it's also a remarkable way to share Shaun's values: the business stems from his experience as a hairdresser and the business is all about hair. So this is actually a very interesting way to make someone feel like they are quickly part of the team and establish a connection to the founder and his story – I know people who follow their hairdresser around from salon to salon, such seems to be the bond between client and hairdresser. Equally, for Shaun, he's getting to know people in the way he knows best: through their hair.

What skills or background stories could you share with employees? One simple way to welcome a new employee if you have already made a Sacred Bundle is simply to sit down with them, explain the Bundle and tell the stories in it. In my sessions with the nine companies I worked with on a one-to-one basis to develop their Bundles, I was very struck at how quickly the Bundles allowed me to get a sense of who they were: their company culture, their core values and important stories. I had worked with hundreds of entrepreneurs and yet the Bundles brought something new to my ability to understand a company's ethos and way of doing business. Their websites and official information did not do this: I could tell you who they were and what they did, but not why and how. So this may be a good way to connect with your new staff. At the same time, you will be clearly showing them that you value stories, that you value honesty and openness – as we've already covered, Bundles are not always 'pretty' – and this can be of use to you in creating a strong and lasting relationship.

Top tip

If you're a leader and you want to share stories both ways with your staff, make your intentions clear. While at Sainsbury's and still young and a bit shy, I noticed that our CEO made a point of eating his lunch in the canteen every day. I think he was probably trying to be approachable and would have liked people to join him. Of course, they didn't: they were too scared to go and sit by him and perhaps be grilled on performance in their department! I wish I had been braver and chatted to him; it would have been interesting. But I also think he should have been clearer about his intentions: perhaps issued a message to say that he would like people to come and talk to him (and maybe reassured them they would not be made to recite sales stats on the spot!). I think, as a leader, he would have benefitted from the opportunities to hear people's stories, as would his staff from having been able to ask questions about company strategy or a future vision. Instead he ate his lunch at an empty table every day, surrounded by tables full of staff, who never approached him. Maybe he was shy too!

Training staff

Here are some ways in which your Sacred Bundle and storytelling more generally can help to welcome, train and develop new staff.

1. Talk new employees through the Bundle when they arrive, so that they are party to the history

of the company and feel as if they were there at its founding.

2.   Suggest that staff create their own Sacred Bundles and ask them to talk you through them. You may find common ground and may find the links between their Bundle and the company Bundle, which explain what drew them to the business in the first place.

3.   Perhaps use the two Bundles for staff appraisals. Look at both and consider: where does the business need to go, and where would the staff member like to move towards, or what do they need help with?

4.   Consider whether staff can add something to the Bundle after they have been with the business for a certain amount of time, perhaps a year.

5.   Send staff on storytelling courses so that they, too, learn the value of storytelling and can add to the storytelling capabilities of your business. Having new staff members regularly return from storytelling courses can refresh and re-energise the whole company's commitment to storytelling.

6.   Keep back some stories to tell that show how you want your staff to behave. If you want them to show outstanding customer care, tell a story where someone did this. If you want them to save money, tell a story about how someone on your team did this. These things are easier

to remember than just instructions on being good to customers and not wasting money. It will make them think more creatively if they can look back at real-life examples rather than a staff manual.

7.   Ask each new employee to become the Keeper of the Bundle until a new staff member arrives. This will make them feel a loyalty and protectiveness to the Bundle and its contents, and allows them to tell some of its stories to a new member of the team.

8.   Ask your team how you can better gather and use stories within the organisation – different people will naturally come up with different ideas which will add to your ability to use storytelling well.

Top Tip

It really helps your business if your staff members are immersed in the stories of your organisation, as well as the stories relating to each individual product. When I worked at retailer Marks & Spencer (M&S), all the staff in the stores only ate M&S food in the staff canteen. The result of this was that if a product was changed in any way, when customers asked where it had gone the staff could tell them that the recipe had been changed, or a better product had been brought in, and could speak with experience about it, having eaten it themselves. Equally, when I was at retailer Sainsbury's, we found out that our organic strawberry farmer used rescue hedgehogs from animal shelters to eat slugs in the strawberry patches rather than pesticides. We shared this story all over social media and on in-store signage, because we recognised that our target consumer would love to know *how* we made our products organic, not just that they *were* organic. It helped that hedgehogs are cute, of course!

17. Bad times and big changes

I discussed moments of change in a business with Sue Hollingsworth. After 22 years at the International School of Storytelling (www.schoolofstorytelling.com), Sue now focuses on true life tales through her own business (www.centreforbiographicalstorytelling.com). With a lot of experience in working with organisations that are facing change, she had some very insightful thoughts around these moments. An entrepreneur may suddenly feel incompetent and uncertain as things change around them and they have to learn new skills, deal with new people, or perhaps fail at something they were certain would succeed. Sue suggested that at these moments it is important for the entrepreneur to consider:

1. Going back to the core story of their business and checking what was important. Was a venture that failed actually because they strayed too far from the core values and goals of the business? Perhaps, perhaps not, but it is worth checking back with your Sacred Bundle and your current product range to see if your customers are flummoxed by a new story you

are telling, that they don't feel fits with the previous one.

2. Frame this part of the story as part of a bigger, longer narrative. Look forwards and consider this a step towards the next, more successful and happy part of the story. Your old story is disappearing, so you need to retell a new one. Consider that in all good fairy stories there are failures, trials and tribulations. There are moments when the hero wanders lost in the forest. And at these moments, our hero is often helped by strangers. What kind of people do you find cropping up in your life at this moment? Are there sidekicks, mentors, a team? What could you learn from them? Do you have something in your Bundle that you might share with them?

3. Ask yourself: what would make you feel safe enough to wander off the main path and learn something new, even if it is a bit scary?

4. Go back to the source of your passion and find the courage to go forwards, as well as the ability to choose people (re-sourcing!) to join you on your journey.

Top Tip

Make some time to tell stories that let go and stories that allow you to grieve, even if just to yourself, but especially if you have a team. Allow time to say goodbye to the old office space, even if it was a dump and your new place is shiny and new: it was still your office and it was there when you first started. Leave time to acknowledge the big order that fell through: don't go all stiff-upper-lipped about it – get everyone to stamp their feet and say 'we hate you for falling through, big order!' or similar. Allow sadness and frustration to come out properly, not be swallowed up.

Then take time to think about your story in a new way: one that allows for what happened and is still a success in the end. Be aware that your time scales are not the world's time scales. Entrepreneurs used to say that they'd done SO MUCH WORK and STILL not got to wherever it was they wanted to get to, and I would end up laughing and pointing out that they'd only been going a year and that they were doing great, and were exactly where I would have expected a promising little business to be. This different perspective on time was often helpful to people.

18. Does your Bundle contain a book?

Books, of course, are a repository for stories. One of the most popular workshops I ran for entrepreneurs at the British Library was called *Books Mean Business*, which looked at how a book could be an important part of a communication strategy for many businesses, no matter what their industry. It's possible that within your Bundle lie the seeds of a book that you can use for greater engagement with your customers. If you're a business, writing a book can help you to get your brand better known, engage with your customers to turn them into your fans, and have something to share on social and traditional media. If you offer services – from coaching to consultancy, architectural skills to running a cleaning business – having a book to your name will help you be seen as an expert and make more clients want to work with you. A book is unlikely to make you a lot of money on its own, but it can position you to make money from it in other ways: e.g. through speaking, consulting, mentoring, training etc. Not all of the reasons below for having a book will apply or appeal to you but some will strike a chord. A book can:

- Get your brand known.

- Be another way to reach new customers; e.g. a cookbook if you are an egg supplier or a café.

- Drive people back to you/your website/your product if they find the book somewhere else (or, for example, if you are at an event/market/conference etc., where someone else has created an audience that you could keep for yourself).

- Create content you can share on your social media and use to hook interest in the traditional media.

- Position you as an expert.

- Make people want to work with you/buy your product.

- Secure customers who cannot (yet) afford your main service (but they might save up for it if they like what they read!).

- Cut out time-wasting questions if you have a lot of these from your existing customers.

- Be used as a calling card: some people hand out their book as a business card to key contacts who are likely to become valuable clients.

- Be used as a free (e-book) 'magnet' to build an email list of customers for your main product or service: you offer the e-book as a freebie to people who, in return, give you their email address.

Key steps to developing a book from your Sacred Bundle

1. Start by asking yourself, what you would use a book for? What do you want a book to do for you? Does it showcase you as an expert? Does it share values or things that inspire you and with which your customer can engage? Does it show how to use your product in greater quantities (recipes for chocolate if you sell chocolate), or how to treat your product carefully (a guide to looking after a bike if you sell bikes)? And so on.

2. Once you are very clear on what the book needs to do, have a look through your Bundle to find some items that might help you out. If you make beautiful clothing and your Bundle contains fabrics from around the world because they inspire you, perhaps a book showcasing amazing fabrics could be for you. If you have a 200-year-old history like Vaughan Memorials, you could create a book showcasing images from funerals around the world through history, or some of the most beautiful headstones you've ever comes across.

3. Do some research. Look at other books in your field. What's missing, or what can you do better? For a long time there were very few recipe books that focused on breakfast. Now there are quite a few as people realised there was a gap in the market. What format are the books in and how long are they? What sort of

style appeals to you? How much do books of this kind cost?

4. Write a basic outline of what the book would include. This gives you a structure to stick to. Ask a few people or even customers for their thoughts on what should be included. Make a list of illustrations or photographs you may wish to include.

5. Write the book. You may be good at this or you may need some help from someone who writes professionally, and who can help you produce the book you want. A few great ideas to engage with your customer-readers are tips, quizzes and diagnostics. You can even ask your readers to engage with you by, for instance, sending in recipes or photos of your product or service in their own lives. This is a story-gathering opportunity. The book should contain a call to action (CTA) that makes the reader do something: sign up for your mailing list; send you a photo; buy more of your product etc. Make sure that you include a well-written author/business biography and contact details.

6. Make sure the book is professionally edited and formatted. The layout should be clear and readable and there should be no errors in the text. Make sure you have a strong title that is clear, without any odd spelling(s) – think of people trying to find it in a search engine – interesting and descriptive. Check that no one

else has the same title: you want to stand out. Make sure you have a clear contents table that doesn't give away all your ideas: I've seen too many books that are something like *100 things to do with kids* and the contents page actually lists all the 100 ideas: why would people buy the book if they can read it all on the preview page?

7. Get a professionally designed cover for the book. Nothing says 'amateur' and is as off-putting as a poorly designed cover. Your book must look and be professional or it will undermine your brand. On that note, make sure it matches your brand; for example, uses the same style and colours as your website.

8. Publish the book. You may want to consider both traditional publishing via a known publisher, or indie (self-)publishing. I'm all for traditional publishing if you can get a publisher excited about your book, but it does have its downsides, most notably:

   i.   an element of luck because no matter how good your book it may just not be 'on trend' right now, or the publisher may already have one that is similar enough to yours not to want another one; and

   ii. the length of time involved in getting a book to market (easily a year and possibly longer).

Indie publishing has its downsides, mainly:

i.   you have to learn quickly and do a lot of work to create a good quality book; and

ii. it will be difficult to get your book into bricks and mortar bookshops.

The main thing going for indie publishing is that you have total control, and it can be fast to get a book to market, so as entrepreneurs are used to having control over their business, indie publishing may suit you better. You can produce e-books as well as paperbacks, which will be printed on-demand – a copy is printed when a person orders it; amazing technology. You can make your books available on Amazon, iBooks, Nook, Kobo, and many more. You will need to set a price (your initial research will help with this). Later on, you could even consider creating an audiobook, via platforms like ACX. If it's just a pdf to give away for free then make sure that it prints well as many people may want to print it out.

Case study: Sharing knowledge brings more (and bigger) customers

Tessa Stuart (www.tessastuart.co.uk) is a food-packaging consultant. She works with hundreds of food and drink entrepreneurs to make sure that their products stand out on the shelf. She wrote and self-published a book called *Packed*, which provides tips to entrepreneurs on how they could improve their packaging, and also gave an insight into the kind of work she does and the services she offers. The book sold well and because of it she was seen as more of an expert than she had been without the book, despite her skills and experience being the same. Consequently, she was invited to speak at various food events, raising her profile and showcasing her to more potential clients. Tessa followed up with a second book, *Flying off the Shelves,* and was promptly offered consultation work with Unilever. Her books made her expertise more visible and resulted in valuable and interesting work opportunities, which of course will only add to her skills and experience going forward.

My own book designers are the team at www.Streetlight-Graphics.com (see Resources) and I can personally recommend their work. You can also look for designers and formatters on Fiverr [www.fiverr.com] and other similar sites, or learn to do this work yourself. However, I would always recommend that your front cover should be done by a professional designer: you can spot the difference a mile away, no matter how good you are creatively.

See the Resources section for useful books, services and organisations.

Exercise

Below is a checklist for starting a book. Ask yourself these questions and you'll be that much closer to creating a book that can help your business grow:

- How would I use a book to grow the business?

135

- What are the books I most admire in this area (e.g. self-help, cooking or architectural design?)

- What are my initial book ideas?

- What resources am I going to need?

- What might hold me back? And how do I address those barriers?

- What are the next five steps I can take towards creating a book?

19. Letting go and saying goodbye

'I almost think I'm going to need professional counselling to get through it, that's how hard it is.' This is what an entrepreneur told me when I asked how it felt having the business grow beyond his own two hands. The business was doing very well and he was pleased, but having new people come into the company and having to let go of total control can be very hard for an entrepreneur. This is not just a business; it is your baby and letting other people take over parts of it can feel almost impossible.

It is worth returning to your Sacred Bundle at this stage. First of all, do you really want the business to grow beyond a certain size? We seem to take it for granted that a business should grow and grow and grow, but what if all you want from the business is to make a decent income for yourself and your family, and to enjoy the freedom and control that comes with owning your own company? I have met too many entrepreneurs who continue to micro-manage their poor employees, unable and unwilling to let go, and who grow more and more unhappy at having to let people into their world. If this is you, take a look at your Sacred Bundle and consider whether you really want the business to grow beyond you, or whether you are happy for it to stay small and within your own two hands.

If you do want to keep the business for yourself then take steps to alter how you run the business. Rather than having people come into the business, you could outsource some tasks – have a virtual assistant; an accountant to do the books; even the manufacturing of your products – and then you can run the business alone if that is what suits you best, although you will need to accept that it cannot grow beyond a certain size. Many entrepreneurs would be happier, I have often felt, if they would accept that this is what they really want, rather than forcing themselves to create a business in which they feel uncomfortable.

However, whereas many entrepreneurs are happy for the business to grow larger and to take people on, they still find the process of letting go very hard. So for those people the Bundle can be used to ritualise and soften the process.

Firstly, look at the Bundle and ask yourself what values it contains, so that you can find people who match or complement them. You will feel more willing to share your baby with people who you feel share your values and your interest in it, just as you might choose a childminder for a real baby because you feel they embody a style of caring for children that you agree with.

Secondly, see if there are ways to share your stories with the people who join you. By going through your Bundle with newcomers and established staff and sharing stories and values – remember to make time to hear their stories and values too – you may find common ground.

Thirdly, you may wish to retell your story to yourself. Until now, your story may have been you against the odds; you all alone and fighting your corner; you the hero on a quest. Now it's time to include more characters in your story. Look back at all the other people you have listed within your bundle. Acknowledge their role in getting you this far, so that you can already begin to see yourself not as the one and only founder of this company, but as part of a group. My young son, learning about 'lead characters' in books at school came home and asked me, 'Who is the lead character in our family?' For once, I had a prompt answer come to mind, rather than thinking of something clever too late. 'There is no lead character in our family,' I said. 'We are an *ensemble*.' Start to change your narrative. You are no longer the lead character. You are part of an ensemble, and there is strength in numbers. Is there something you can add to the bundle to acknowledge this change? Can you invent a new ritual to acknowledge the team that you are building: everyone out for lunch together on pay day; special biscuits for the weekly team meeting; funny hats for people's birthdays etc.? You need something that acknowledges that there is now more than one of you.

The other time when an entrepreneur has to let go is a bit more final: when they sell the company and move on. Again, this can be hard and you can use your Bundle to capture and help to ease this transition. If the new owner is the kind of person to understand the Bundle, perhaps you could have a ritual where you tell them the stories contained in it one last time, perhaps add a final item to the Bundle and drink a toast to its continued future and then gift the Bundle to them. Or, if they are not that way inclined, you might want to take the Bundle with you and allow it to form a memento of the past, perhaps displaying it somewhere that gives you pleasure. Claire from Upcycliste was about to make major changes to her life and work and found the process of creating her Sacred Bundle a positive chance to look back at the business so far and be proud of it, before stepping into the next phase of her entrepreneurial journey.

Top Tip

There may be some data that you are trying to get across – numbers or information of some sort that you want people to retain – and you may be wondering how to get this into your presentation if you're supposed to be storytelling. Try to reshape it in human terms. A company I worked for gave out government grants and we were trying to show how successful those grants were in changing businesses. We worked out that in the course of a year the grants had enabled over 180 new jobs to be created. But we tried to phrase it in more human terms: every other day, someone started a new job because of these grants. The exact number is not such a big deal, but the impact on people's lives is.

20. A WARNING

There was once a poor farmer who had a goose, which one day, as if by magic, laid a golden egg. The farmer and his wife were ecstatic. They sold the golden egg and were grateful for the money, which would allow them to fix their leaking roof. The next day, the goose laid another golden egg. Again, the farmer and his wife were very happy. Now they could afford a new pair of strong oxen rather their weary old donkey to plough the land. The next day, they waited with bated breath, and sure enough, the goose laid a golden egg.

'We will be rich!' they cried. 'The goose will lay a golden egg every day!' Then they thought: Why should we wait for many days to pass to get the golden eggs? If we kill the goose now, we can have all the golden eggs at once! *They hurried to kill the goose and having done so opened it up – but alas, the goose was like any*

> *other goose inside and there was no sign*
> *of any gold at all!*

This story, from *Aesop's Fables*, is why I chose the image on the front cover of this book. A golden egg is something magical; something that you would tell stories about. But it also contains a warning: you have to use stories carefully, with honesty and authenticity. Fail to do this and you will kill the goose that lays the golden egg. Below are some ways in which you might kill the golden goose. Steer clear of them!

Not following through with your storytelling commitment

This applies to those companies that already have a fair number of staff in them. If you commit publicly to developing a storytelling culture but staff then find that your enthusiasm wanes after a brief period, the culture will die out pretty quickly. Stories shared need to be praised and new opportunities for storytelling need to be welcomed with open arms, rather than dismissing them because there isn't time at the end of a long meeting, or other things are 'more important'.

Perhaps you can appoint a 'storyteller' role in the business that gets moved round on a monthly basis, whereby that person needs to protect and promote the importance of storytelling: making sure stories have their own place on meeting agendas; coming up with new storytelling activities; or ensuring the website is stocked with stories. Allow staff to challenge any attempts to downgrade the importance of storytelling. The culture will take a while to develop and it needs time to embed itself. During that time it needs a protector, a Knight Errant, to shield it from harm.

Top Tip

Look back at what you promised story-telling-wise for your business culture. Are you sticking to it? Has 'Storytelling Friday' been lost along the way, or have 'Monday Customer Tales' disappeared? Do you need a storytelling bodyguard? Appoint someone to haul you back on track. If you took on too much at once, admit it and start small again. Small and committed is better than huge and forgotten.

Only picking stories that sound PR-friendly

It can be tempting to choose information or stories about your company that you think are PR-friendly but in which you have little real interest. You may have lived on a houseboat for a period as a child and think that this will be a good story to put on your website or to trot out in a pitch when you realise that a lot of your customers seem to like boats, and are buying your products. But if you actually suffer from seasickness and hated the houseboat period of your childhood because you were certain a crocodile lived somewhere nearby and it frightened you, then this story is not one you should use. Yes, it's PR-friendly, but it's not true to you at all. You could, of course, use the story in a funny way: to admit that you hate boats and isn't it ironic that lots of your customers are sailing enthusiasts and keep offering you boat trips. This would be a much better way of using the story.

Top Tip

Take a look through the stories you read about other companies in your industry: many of them may sound familiar because they try to emulate the top brand's cute, made-for-PR story. Don't go there. Be different. Think about what sets your company apart, not how you can shape your story to fit a common mould.

Don't lose authenticity through overly slick media

Many company websites use stock photos of people discussing ideas or making presentations. They explain that their team is very creative, that it comes up with amazing solutions to problems – and then illustrate that with a stock image of an actor leaping in the air with balloons or whatever. This is not authentic. If you think your team really is creative and amazing, then get some photos of them doing creative, amazing and even downright silly things. If you are proud that your team regularly does volunteering together, then use images or videos of them doing just that, rather than using actors to portray it. If you genuinely know the growers of your coffee beans and care about them then don't use a stock photo of a coffee-bean grower: use the pictures you took when you visited them and had a drink together. Yes, your footage will be less professional and your photos may be a bit grainy, but they will be real and authentic and your customers will engage far more strongly with them as a result.

Top Tip

Take a good look at your website and other social media. Are your images professional? Good. Are they a bit too slick? Not so good. Try not to use stock images of 'business' people: use your own people, even if you need to bring in a photographer to make the images look professional. A picture taken from your office window of a rainbow will be more authentic than a stock rainbow picture. Set up a competition for great images of your products or people. You never know, your customers might surprise you with their photographic talents!

Avoid developing a culture of horror stories

When you develop a culture of sharing stories, it's very easy to start sharing negative stories as well as positive stories: the horror stories of dreadful customers; the blame stories that proliferate easily in corporate culture; the warning stories of bad things happening to good people. Make it clear that you want to make space for the positive stories to really shine. Praise stories for their great outcomes or good intentions; tell stories about customers who were appreciative; and (even better) those who started off tricky but were won round by a colleague's charm and perseverance in offering good service. However, don't just dismiss all negative stories, because you can then risk them being told in corners and huddles and undermining your positive story culture. Find a way to get them out in the open.

Top Tip

If there are true horror stories to be told, tell them once with full dramatic staging. Find a way to learn something from them and 'send them on their way' with a round of applause rather than letting them be told over and over again in whispers. In this way you can maintain a genuine positive atmosphere rather than letting an unwanted 'shadow side' of storytelling develop.

Don't get *too* expert in your delivery

During the fundraising television programme *Sport Relief,* my husband and I watched the experienced presenter Clare Balding struggle as she told the story of children sleeping on the streets in Africa. She delivered an impassioned speech to the camera, full of dreadful facts and figures that she must have spent time committing to memory. My husband and I, tucked up in our warm bed watching TV, our own children safely asleep in the next room, nodded sadly at the points she was making and the enormity of the situation.

Then something changed. Perhaps because of the true emotion she was feeling, she stumbled over her prepared words and we saw her try to express what she was feeling in seeing these children for herself. Her own words came out of her, both awkward and true. 'These are not bad children,' she said. 'These could be your children, sleeping here on the streets.' My husband and I picked up our phones in unison and donated to the charity within five minutes of her saying this. It wasn't that we hadn't understood the facts and figures she had so diligently rehearsed and offered, it was that, in using her own words, Clare had suddenly taken us to stand by her side and look down on children who could have been ours. She made us feel the horror of our own children lying there, vulnerable and cold, because her own feelings had been expressed. The facts and figures should have moved us but they just didn't have the same impact. When we made the donations, we were trying to get our own children off the street to somewhere warm and safe.

Top Tip

It can be easy to tell a story so many times that you learn it by rote, that you say what ought to be said, with all the right facts and figures, using heart-tugging images and the correct delivery or presentation style... but somehow it has little impact. Sometimes you need to *feel* the story and allow the words to stumble out. This applies whether you are a charity or a commercial business. If you've told and retold a story and you think it's become a little stale, try and really feel it again and see if different, clumsier words come out which tell the story better. Twice in the course of making Sacred Bundles the founders cried when sharing why their work was important to them, and the impact on me was huge It made their commitment to what they were doing seem far greater than all the previous information they had given me. Don't be afraid to show feelings. Feelings are human.

Don't share the bad stuff

While it is good to be honest and upfront about bad things that may have happened while telling stories, be aware that being rude about past employees, customers and competitors is not a good idea. It will make you look bad for not handling situations better and will lead people to wonder whether you will be complaining about *them* the next time you tell the story. Try to stay focused on the positives: if you had a difficult customer but turned the situation around; if you had an employee who you struggled with but is now one of your most loyal and important team members; if you were battling against a competitor but then learnt to work together for mutual benefit – these stories will all show you in a much better light. So, don't share the bad stuff unless you have learnt from it.

Top Tip

Think about any bad moments in your business story so far. What did you learn from each? Be careful of the language you use: 'I learnt not trust people so easily' is still negative, whereas 'I have learnt to take my time getting to know people before developing a long-lasting relationship – and to have some safeguards in place' is still true, but is more positive.

Beware of the story the world is telling *you*

We've established that storytelling is powerful. So be aware of its power over *you*, as well as your stories' power over others. I'd like you to look back at the Sacred Bundle of Desi Doll (the first case study in chapter 8). I admire Farzana, because she has not allowed the 'entrepreneur' story to force the choices she makes. The entrepreneur story with which we are all familiar is: plucky person comes up with great idea, works very hard, gets wonderful investment/investor or massive sales order, makes it big and grows to a gigantic world-leading business. I could point to many of these stories and you would recognise them.

But I have met many, many entrepreneurs who actually just want to run their business on a small scale. They want to work by themselves, perhaps with the odd member of staff for specific tasks or busy moments. They want to enjoy the freedom of making their own choices and choosing their own hours. They want to make a decent income, but they don't *really* want to be millionaires because they value something else (usually family, a social life, the time spent practising their craft etc.). *But* many of these people force themselves to grow bigger, take on staff (even though they clearly hate managing them and dislike losing control of the business), work all hours of the day and night, to get other people to make their product (even though they enjoyed the process of making their products)… *because* this is the entrepreneurial 'story' they have been told and read countless times, and they believe in it.

So take a look at that story or others you are told about running your own business and then take a look at what you really want from your business or organisation. Do they match? Because you are free to write your own story.

21. Happy storytelling!

Thank you for reading this book, I hope you will find it useful as you move along your entrepreneurial journey. If you need to learn more, then the next section on Resources will help you. These are books and websites from a range of fantastic storytellers, whose books I have on my own shelves, and whose thoughts and stories I have found fascinating. Do explore them as you grow in confidence and are ready to take storytelling to the next level.

In the meantime, have confidence in your ability to use stories within your own business. You've known about the power of storytelling since you were a small child… you can do this!

Resources

This section is a combination of books and websites that you might find useful as you develop your storytelling skills. I've put a little bit of information about each.

Books

Below are some titles that I have chosen from the seventy or more that I went through in the research stage for this book. I hope you find them useful, if you'd like to read more deeply about a particular topic. They are the books I went out and bought for myself.

Denning, Stephen. 2011. *The Leader's Guide to Storytelling* (John Wiley). For people learning leadership skills and wanting to use storytelling as a leader, this is a great book. Denning covers choosing the right story for the challenge, key elements of storytelling performance and what to use stories for, from neutralising gossip or rumour to encouraging collaboration.

Dietz, Karen and Silverman, Lori L. 2014. *Business Storytelling for Dummies* (John Wiley). A good overview on the subject and an introduction to many of the big names in business storytelling.

Duarte, Nancy. 2010. *Resonate* (John Wiley). A very different way to present your information. Forget boring PowerPoint slides, Nancy offers a new look at how to get your message across and 'present visual stories that transform audiences'.

Haven, Kendall. 2007. *Story Proof* (Libraries Unlimited). If you'd like to read up on why stories work and the proof behind those reasons, then I recommend this book. Haven is a researcher and a storyteller and what he finds is that thousands of original sources all agree on one thing: storytelling works.

Hollingsworth, Sue and Ramsden, Ashley. 2013. *The Storyteller's Way* (Hawthorn Press). From the International School of Storytelling (*www.schoolofstorytelling.com*), this is a very practical book for developing your storytelling skills, from voice and posture to 'putting the flesh on the bones' of a story. It is a great book to work through (the school also offers courses from one day to three months in length). It is also full of exercises to develop your abilities.

Karmel, Annabel. 2015. *Mumpreneur* (Vermilion). This book offers good quality business advice for any entrepreneur, but what really makes it stand out for me is that all the case studies feature women and mothers. It is rare for a business book to focus on women so strongly and for this reason it can be a source of uplifting stories and inspiration for entrepreneurs who are also women and mothers.

Le Guin, Ursula K. 1989. *Dancing at the Edge of the World* (Grove Press). This includes a number of fascinating articles on writing and storytelling, including *The Carrier Bag Theory of Fiction,* in which she looks at the difference between heroic hunter stories and the everyday minutiae of gatherer stories.

Mead, Geoff. 2014 *Telling the Story* (John Wiley). As well as making many good points showing how stories can be used, Mead includes a very helpful section on some of the practicalities of storytelling.

Neuhauser, Peggy. 1993. *Corporate Legends & Lore* (McGraw-Hill). This is the book that first suggested Sacred Bundles to me, and Neuhauser is excellent at viewing corporations through a different lens, made up of different tribes with their own legends. It is perhaps more applicable to larger organisations, but still very interesting. You may have to find it second-hand on Amazon or similar. Peggy is now retired but her thinking was really useful to me in developing the process of Sacred Bundles.

Pink, Daniel. 2014. *To Sell is Human* (Canongate). Pink's book focuses on how to make a sale, and he includes a 'Pixar' pitch for selling, which uses a story structure to create interest and engagement for your product or service.

Sachs, Jonah. 2012. *Winning the Story Wars: Why Those Who Tell and Live the Best Stories Will Rule the Future*

(Harvard Business Review Press). Sachs talks about us now being in a *digitoral* society, where we are returning to the traditions of oral storytelling but through digital mediums. He has a lot of examples of when marketing materials go viral on social media and why those stories broke through.

Silverman, Lori. 2008. *Wake me up when the Data is Over* (John Wiley). An interesting look at how many different organisations already use storytelling for myriad purposes.

Simmons, Annette. 2006. *The Story Factor* (Basic Books; 2nd revised edition). Simmons uses over 100 stories to show the impact they can have in different settings, and includes a lot of useful pointers on everything from body language to using all the senses when storytelling.

Vaynerchuk, Gary. 2013. *Jab, Jab, Jab, Right Hook* (HarperBusiness). A really interesting look at how to tell your stories on the most popular social-media platforms, with multiple visual examples of what works and what doesn't. Very readable.

Creating a Book

Services:

If you end up writing a book for your business, here are two very good services I use:

- *Streetlight Graphics www.streetlightgraphics. com*

Streetlight Graphics do book cover design as well as interior formatting for both e-books and paperback. They have a very clear pricing structure and are great to work with.

- *Winskill Editorial www.winskilleditorial.co.uk*

Gale at Winskill Editorial is an experienced editor who can help you improve your book, from considering structural changes and smoothing your text to proofreading.

Books:

Some very useful titles:

- Eager, Rob. 2012. *Sell Your Book Like Wildfire* (Writer's Digest Books).

- Penn, Joanna. 2013. *How to Market a Book* (CreateSpace).

- Sambuchino, Chuck. 2012. *Create Your Writer Platform* (Writer's Digest Books).

Organisations:

- The Alliance of Independent Authors (www. allianceindependentauthors.org) is worth checking out, as it supports self-published authors and offers a lot of good advice in its archives of articles on the subject, from sorting out ISBNs to marketing the finished product.

Storytellers to learn from

Sue Hollingsworth, www.centreforbiographicalstorytelling. com
Sue works and performs all over the world and after 22 years at the International School of Storytelling is now creating her own business focused on true life tales including leadership stories.

Hannah McDowall, Twitter: @storyhannah or hannahmcdowall@gmail.com
Hannah has worked for many years with social entrepre-neurs and now works as a storyteller and a drawer-out of other people's tales, including the elderly.

Elaine Powell, www.elainepowell.com
Elaine is an international speaker, public speaking coach and TEDx curator. She works with entrepreneurs, business owners to improve their confidence and presentation skills for business, pitching and storytelling, through seminars, workshops and private coaching.

Maddi Riddell at ?What If! www.whatifinnovation.com
?What If! is an innovation agency working on everything from brands to new product development.

Paul Wilson at Make Believe, www.makebelieveuk.com
Make Believe works to develop consumer and health-care brands based on storytelling.

Talks on storytelling

I love TED Talks and you can learn so much from them. Take a look at some of these and be inspired! (www.ted.com/talks):

- JJ Abrams: The Mystery Box
- Tyler Cowen: Be suspicious of simple stories
- Nancy Duarte: Uncovering the Structure of the Greatest Communicators
- Raghava KK: Shake up your story
- Raghava KK: What's your 200-year plan?
- Frans Lanting: The story of life in photographs
- Rob Legato: The Art of Creating Awe
- Joe Sabia: The Technology of Storytelling
- Andrew Stanton: The Clues to a Great Story

Also keep an eye on Lyn Graft's developing site (www.storytellingforentrepreneurs.com), which will use the experience he's had filming the founding stories of over 500 entrepreneurs to offer insights and online courses for entrepreneurs wanting to hone their skills.

The British Library's Business & IP Centre (BIPC)

This is where I was based as a Writer in Residence for most of 2016. Before that, I had spent time there, giving workshops and meeting entrepreneurs, in part, so that I could introduce them to what the BIPC could offer them at all different stages of their business journey. If you can't make it to London, then there are eight National

Network Centres around the UK, housed in other key libraries. I highly recommend a visit.

The BIPC supports small business owners, entrepreneurs and inventors. The centre, with a networking area and its own Reading Room, is open six days a week with its own team to help you take the right steps to start up, protect and grow your business.

You can develop your ideas with their market research and company databases. I was shocked to discover how much Mintel reports cost – we're talking thousands – and you can access them there for free. In addition, you can learn new skills at free and subsidised workshops or mini-masterclasses, have a confidential one-to-one with business experts and put your questions to some of the UK's most successful entrepreneurs at their inspiring talks. There's an event on almost every day and the Reading Room is full of great materials that cover pretty much any industry you can think of.

www.bl.uk/business-and-ip-centre

Your Free Book

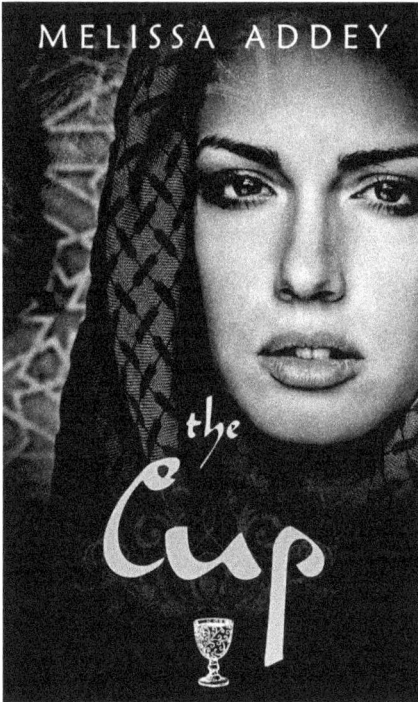

The city of Kairouan in Tunisia, 1020. Hela has powers too strong for a child – both to feel the pain of those around her and to heal them. But when she is given a mysterious cup by a slave woman, its powers overtake her life, forcing her into a vow she cannot hope to keep. So begins a quartet of historical novels set in Morocco as the Almoravid Dynasty sweeps across Northern Africa and Spain, creating a Muslim Empire that endured for generations.

Download your free copy at
www.melissaaddey.com

www.ingramcontent.com/pod-product-compliance
Lightning Source LLC
Chambersburg PA
CBHW030520210326
41597CB00013B/974